What people are saying about
ENHANCE Employee Engagement:

"*Every business leader will gain from Nicole Mason's exceptional insights into organizational productivity and employee morale.* ENHANCE Employee Engagement *provides a proven framework and specific tools that help companies to stand the test of time and thrive.*"

—MARSHALL GOLDSMITH
author of the *New York Times* and global bestseller
What Got You Here Won't Get You There.

"*Nicole has made a direct hit on the strategic thought and conversation today to ensure relevance tomorrow of your organization and for yourself. I have consulted, written and researched this for twenty years, this is a must read work!*"

—DR. JEFFREY MAGEE, CMC, PDM, CSP
Human Capital Developer & Best Selling Author, and Publisher,
Performance/P360 Magazine, www.ProfessionalPerformanceMagazine.com

ENHANCE
Employee
Engagement

Future Proof Company Strategies

Nicole B. Mason

True North Press

Fremont, California

ENHANCE Employee Engagement
Future Proof Company Strategies

Nicole B. Mason

True North Press

PO Box 545, Fremont, CA 94537

www.truenorthpress.org

ISBN: 978-0-9861318-0-6
Library of Congress Control Number: 2015902268

Book Design: Peri Poloni-Gabriel, Knockout Design,
www.knockoutbooks.com

First Edition, 2015
Published in the United States of America

To my son,
whose presence and importance continually
give me a healthy perspective on work and life.
You and your peers are the employers and
employees of the future.

CONTENTS

ABOUT THE AUTHOR

NICOLE MASON is an experienced corporate strategist and recovering corporate attorney who founded Omnivantage Business Professionals, a growth change management and diversity consulting and training firm. After nearly 20 years of applying her skills to a variety of roles at several Silicon Valley based companies, including Sun Microsystems (Oracle) and Metricom (Ricochet), and navigating corporate politics and job changes to climb the corporate ladder, Nicole exited corporate employment after her son was born. As the General Counsel of a NASDAQ listed cloud services company, she witnessed and experienced situations that frequently hinder recruitment, retention and collaboration in most corporations. As a direct result, Nicole now assists companies in creating sustainable workplace cultures and best practices that are both lucrative and socially responsible.

Nicole applies her intuitive knack for identifying root causes, and broad-based knowledge, to solve the most vexing and persistent productivity challenges for companies of all sizes. She firmly believes corporations that provide professional growth opportunities and balanced lifestyles for employees are also more profitable, innovative and enduring. Nicole's results oriented services and interactive trainings help her clients overcome the internal communication and employee engagement challenges most companies face today, and will increasingly struggle with in the future.

Having worked with colleagues and managed employees in offices all around the world, Nicole has extensive experience successfully managing remote employees and providing support across time zones, as well as communicating across cultures and collaborating with a variety of organizational functional groups. She not only appreciates diversity, but also fully understands its benefits and knows how to maximize the untapped synergies.

Nicole is a licensed attorney with the State Bar of California and an active member of a number of professional organizations. Many of her trainings are certified for CLE and HR CE credits.

For more information, visit www.employeeandclientengagement.com

ACKNOWLEDGEMENTS

THIS BOOK WOULD NOT be possible without the support of my loving and helpful husband. Thank you, Anuj, for enabling me to carve out the time to write this, and for your invaluable input on its content. The Mission Publishing team, especially Jill Cheeks, were also instrumental in helping me complete this book and get it published. Thank you, Jill, for providing a wealth of insightful guidance and feedback, based on your HR expertise and extensive book writing and publishing experience.

Additional thanks to my clients, all of whom put their trust in me and contributed their insights and experiences utilizing the framework and tactics described in this book. Decades of in-house legal and business experience working as an employee for corporations ranging from start-ups to mature multi-nationals, and research into workplace studies, diversity issues and generational attitudes, enrich this book.

I take this opportunity to express gratitude to all of my colleagues and managers who mentored, supported and promoted me over the years, as well as those who professionally challenged me, exposed me to a range of corporate realities, and ultimately created opportunities for me to hone my "soft" skills and expand my management acumen. With their guidance, assistance and the opportunities they provided, I was able to rise up the corporate ranks as a female employee in Silicon Valley and have a successful career for which I am eternally grateful. The fulfilling, educational and colorful anecdotes from all of my corporate experiences inspired this book and the work I do today.

Thanks to the timely and widely available studies and surveys conducted by the renowned consulting firms and institutions I cite, this book also includes lessons learned from best practices across all industries. I greatly appreciate the awareness generated by other writers, professors, executives and organizations with a keen interest and passion for the topics covered in this book.

These acknowledgements would not be complete without recognizing my gifted editor Aden Nichols, of Little Fire Editorial, for polishing this book with his review and edits. Kudos and big thanks to Peri Gabriel of Knockout Design for the design touches. This book also benefited from the contributions of several friends and colleagues, including Rod Stilwell and Tabitha Bedoukian. I am so grateful for the encouragement, support and enthusiasm of the many other friends and business associates who cheered me on, anxiously awaited this book's publication and shared their thoughts about the value of its content—thank you. I feel extremely fortunate and grateful for the attention, encouragement and endorsements received from Marshall Goldsmith, author of the New York Times and global bestseller *What Got You Here Won't Get You There,* and Dr. Jeffrey Magee CMC, PDM, CSP, Human Capital Developer & Best Selling Author and Publisher, *Performance/P360 Magazine.* Finally, thanks to everyone else that reads and recommends this book to others.

INTRODUCTION

Employee Engagement Greases the Skids for Enduring Success

WHAT IS "ENGAGEMENT"? *Merriam-Webster* says it is "emotional involvement or commitment," also "the state of being in gear." As it pertains to employee performance, engagement is capturing their thoughts and feelings around the clock, by inspiring them to view your work as part of their driving purpose. Organizations that do not engage their employees, in a manner that causes them to care about the company, will fail.

Engagement, by its nature, grabs people emotionally; it transcends distractions and concerns to motivate people to focus, and push *themselves* to a higher level of action. It is also an elusive, complex concept that means different things to different people; engagement can be difficult to measure with precision and certainty. As a consequence, very few managers and organizations "do" engagement well, but we all know engagement when we see it. We can also sense when it is lacking or missing entirely. This book provides clarity and offers solutions that demystify employee engagement so you—as a manager and leader—can successfully foster a culture that engages the minds, hearts, and greatest talents of your employees.

Wouldn't it be great to work with people who are committed and excited about their role advancing your company's mission and vision? Imagine what your organization could accomplish with everyone working together and giving their absolute best. Imagine the positive impact generated by a company that withstands the test of time, delivering products and services that improve people's lives for generations to come. Employee engagement is fuel for the innovation, adaptability, collaboration, and collective effort required to sustain the momentum that will ensure your company's prosperity and legacy.

Simply stated, the human resources department (HR) is not and cannot be responsible for employee engagement.

Engagement is foundational to the sustained success of any business venture, with respect to customers *and* employees. While the vast majority of companies acknowledge employees and customers equally as their most important assets, far more resources are devoted to effectively engaging with customers. Marketing departments have budgets and goals dedicated to customer engagement; very few companies commit similar resources and focus to employee engagement. While HR is often concerned with employee policies, satisfaction and benefits, it is not dedicated to employee engagement. Simply stated, the human resources department (HR) is not and cannot be responsible for employee engagement. Employee engagement is the responsibility of every manager and employee in an organization, especially company executives. Short-changing and giving short-shrift to employee engagement is a problem that typically costs thousands—even tens of thousands—of dollars *per employee*, and those are just the direct out-of-pocket costs associated with losing a good employee. That figure does not include the incalculable costs of countless missed opportunities and lost revenues caused by employee turnover, errors, lack of diligence, damage to reputation, and absenteeism. So doesn't it make sense for employee engagement to be a priority for your executives and managers?

Employee engagement is the solution to costly and debilitating lackluster employee performance, as well as talent acquisition and retention problems. The bottom line to achieving this holy grail of business happiness is to task a cross-functional group, or individuals within each department, of your organization solely with becoming educated about all things affecting employee performance and implementing policies, processes and ongoing programs that gain the mind share of your employees. Employees expect more from employers today—that is a fact. And that reality needs to be embraced rather than discounted as an "entitled millennial" problem, or other issue de jour, that gets avoided or is mistakenly believed will simply go away. Employees will continue to demand more freedom and flexibility.

On the flip side, today's employers expect more from their employees than in years past. Smartphones and tablets, extreme connectivity, and the break-neck pace enabled by digital technology reset expectations of what is possible (and necessary) and skew the perception of time. Minutes now feel like hours when waiting for a response to an e-mail. However, unlike machines, human resources are not entirely replaceable and they are exhaustible—and employees today, especially the high performers, know it. The most creative, dependable, and productive employees expect to be valued and acknowledged in meaningful ways. For this reason, employee engagement is more important now than ever before.

Over the past two decades, I have witnessed changes in employees' attitudes, as well as monumental shifts in business and the world itself. The methods that worked to acquire, motivate, and retain employees even a few years ago do not work well today and will not work at all as more of the so-called "Millennials" begin their climb up the proverbial corporate ladder and Gen Z enters the workforce. The post-9/11 and Great Recession world has generated widespread social disruption. Established ways of thinking and accepted "truths" are now constantly questioned and often rejected, and people's expectations and ways of communicating are evolving as well. The essence of these changes, as they relate to employees, is best expressed by the term "work–life integration."

Where people used to talk about "work–life balance," the conversation has shifted to a more holistic, non-compartmentalized view of life. Work is no longer a 9 to 5 proposition; indeed, it isn't even necessarily a single block of time that can be neatly carved out from the rest of the day. Employees at all levels are regularly expected to work outside these conventional daytime hours, or they need to do so to fulfill their personal and professional obligations. Changing demographics, which include more single parents and fewer stay-at-home parents, result in increased demands on employees' time during the day. Other societal changes also contribute to an overall need and expectation of greater flexibility in work schedules, and an expanding array of digital tools facilitates this occupational malleability. Ironically, these same technological advances mold employees' expectations regarding availability and productivity. There must be a bit of give and take. Work is increasingly encroaching upon people's lives outside the corporate workplace in the evening, over the weekend—even during vacations and holidays. To secure and retain good employees, a manager or employer must acknowledge and respect this fact. The best employees are engaged employees: the ones who love what they do, deliver the most value to their employers, and view work as part of their identity and life.

As a business oriented lawyer with decades of experience working in -house at technology and telecommunications companies, wearing many different hats over the years, I have lived and worked through tumultuous changes in the business world. I was identified as a high-performing employee and I hired other employees and managed teams, all around the globe. I reported to traditionalists, baby boomers and fellow Gen Xers, and managed baby-boomers, other Gen Xers, and Gen Y "millennials." I learned to adapt to the shifting and ever-increasing demands employers placed on my colleagues and me, and modified my own requirements of employers and managers accordingly. As a conscientious employee, I managed my career proactively. When I found myself disengaged or de-motivated at a company, I voted with my feet to avail myself of opportunities offered by a new employer. Ultimately, I opted out of employment in favor of entrepreneurship, like so many of today's high-performing employees do. Based on my conversations with hundreds of high performing and experienced employees, as well as others' studies and surveys of thousands of employees which are referenced throughout this book, it is obvious that *engagement is the key ingredient* in acquiring, motivating, and retaining top-flight employees.

Even companies recognized as great places to work have individual employees, workgroups, or entire departments that are simply disengaged. Common sense, reinforced by verifiable data, suggests that what engages one person will not engage another; engagement triggers are subjective and vary from person to person. High turnover in a particular group, or company-wide, is a classic telltale symptom of an engagement problem. As a manager or leader you must understand the wants, needs, ambitions, and life circumstances of your employees, not only to motivate them, but to also gain their loyalty and mindshare. Your organization is a reflection of *you*.

The fact is, effective management of personnel is a learned skill. While some individuals may seem like "born managers" or "born leaders" because of some natural talents they have in the area of people skills or decision-making ability, nobody is born knowing everything one needs to know to successfully manage and lead people. Likewise, someone who is excellent at performing a function as an individual contributor is not automatically qualified to manage others performing that same function; *doing* is different from *managing*. There is also distinction between managing and leading, and engagement requires both. Leaders motivate people temporarily with their vision. Managers are tasked with sustaining that motivation and channeling it to achieve specific results that help accomplish the mission. To do that, managers must lead to some extent. Conversely, leaders must manage others to build and maintain a team to help execute their plan. You cannot expect an innovative or interesting endeavor to keep people engaged all by itself.

Really engaging employees requires you to be educated in particular skills and employ them consistently to earn trust and gain influence and respect.

This book is inspired by what I witnessed and experienced inside companies, including Fortune 500 multinationals, established midsized companies, and start-ups, in a wide range of industries over the past twenty years. I believe corporations are beneficial for society. A team of people working together towards a common goal can always accomplish more than any single individual. In its highest and best form, a corporation can provide wonderful careers and lifestyles for employees and opportunities for people to do good and meaningful work, *and* profitably sell and deliver useful products and services to customers. People are the contributors, leaders, and drivers of every company's vision and mission, and engagement is the human element that sparks their best possible performance and results.

People do not inherently know how to bring out the best in others while managing conflicts that naturally arise under a variety of circumstances. It is not easy to align people with different opinions, personalities, and perspectives to work together in harmony and synergy to accomplish a big goal or ongoing mission. Handling conflict management well is key to engaging employees. Unresolved or avoided conflicts distract and disengage people. Conflicts arise for many understandable reasons. Great ideas and stronger relationships often come out of discovering the root of the conflicts and working through them. It is also important to follow certain practices to foster a positive and productive environment, while balancing the needs and wants of a variety of people and priorities. This exploration of employee engagement provides guidance in these areas to help you develop and maintain high-performing team dynamics. Also included are resources from management training and leadership development courses to enable you to practice and master these culture-creating skills.

Cultures evolve to survive; those that do not morph with the times die. Corporations are like societies, each with a unique culture that both supports and reflects the values of its people as a group. We have all seen societal values shift over time, and regardless of how we may feel about those changes we must acknowledge them. Ignoring changes you do not like will not make them disappear; it will only serve to generate problems until you stand up and take corrective action. Like societies, corporations must change with the times to stay relevant and competitive. Change does not require throwing out everything that exists and starting from scratch. On the contrary, the most beneficial changes are incremental, like updates based on feedback and lessons learned over time and through experience. That is why this book is titled *ENHANCE Employee Engagement,* referencing an acronym of the elements critical to boosting profits through better employee relations.

The only corporations that will grow and sustain themselves today and in the future are the ones with leaders and managers driving cultures that incorporate employee engagement. Culture is not just a set of values and policies—it is a daily habit that amounts to a way of doing everything throughout the organization. Policies, procedures, employee benefits and perks, the physical work environment, daily interactions, corporate events and programs, as well as internal communications must all send a consistent and clear message in support of the culture you intend and desire—the culture that will enable your company to achieve its objectives. It goes without saying that your vision, mission, and style as a leader lays the foundation for your company's culture—but a foundation is not a building, nor is it a culture.

Culture is a context that attracts specific types of people, so it is important to ensure your culture is a good fit for the types of people you want to attract and retain. Communications and daily interactions between management and employees, departments, and peers simultaneously reflect and shape the culture of an organization. Your company's culture is an integral component of its reputation with customers and employees alike. Therefore it is something to protect, value, and invest in if you want to sustain teams that will support your goals and customers who will perpetually generate profits. Sustaining success, growth, or innovation requires the right culture.

By its nature, culture maintains a focus on the human element and mirrors what is occurring while attracting more of the same. For example, when I was an employee of a corporation with a reputation for being "cool, innovative, and disruptive" (in a good way), I noticed it attracted talented people who really cared about the company's mission, passionately worked long hours, and were loyal advocates of the company. However when I worked for a company whose employees were disengaged, there was constant turmoil and poor execution, and none of management's strategies got implemented. I've also worked at companies where there were mixed levels of engagement. Hiring and managing people in all of these environments taught me a lot about engagement. Along the way, I observed and learned what worked and what did not work in getting teams to collaborate effectively. Out of these experiences, I developed practices, systems, and tools that promoted high levels of commitment. This generated a kind of tenacity and creativity that facilitated efforts above and beyond the call of duty and produced amazing results. The friendships, respect, flexibility, and trust between everyone on these teams supported individual high performance and produced excellent outcomes for the company. *Culture, performance,* and *engagement* are three inseparable elements of leadership and management.

Strategies targeted at perpetuating a high-performance culture specific and unique to your organization are key to successfully reshaping employee engagement. Putting those strategies into practice is a team effort: no one person or position is responsible—everyone has a role to play. Strategies, programs, and practices that worked to yield high performance and engender loyalty ten or more years ago simply do not work today, and will not work in the foreseeable future. Moreover, these time-honored methods incorporate common beliefs and behaviors that can actually *undermine* employee engagement. Various chapters in this book address common myths and missteps concerning employee engagement, and well-intentioned but defective practices that get in the way of driving high performance throughout your organization. The initial chapter lays out in detail all of the parts comprising a complete road map of employee engagement that accurately leads to more profits and productivity. From there, I will use the employee engagement road map to take you on a tour with stops along the way that explain how you can build, implement, and sustain a successful high-performance culture at your company right now.

In this book you will discover new ways of attracting, motivating, and keeping employees—regardless of their generation or function—these approaches vastly improve productivity and morale. You will come to understand and appreciate why it is crucial to partner with your employees. You will also walk away with a flexible framework to apply to generating, enhancing and maintaining engagement in your particular organization. Most leaders and managers intuitively know that engaged employees are important, even crucial, to their company's success, but somehow this gets lost in translation and overlooked in the day-to-day execution of goals, policies and initiatives. Most companies take time to develop corporate values and create some sort of company culture, but fail to tie that to every employee's role and daily responsibilities and, consequently, employees miss the point and a huge engagement opportunity is lost. This book bridges those gaps. The critically important take away you will gain from this book is insight into how much your employees' engagement impacts your company's bottom line—and what you can do to harness their untapped energy to drive awesome results!

Chapter 1

DRIVEN INSPIRATION

Employee Engagement Is The Road to Higher Profits

THE ESSENCE OF EMPLOYEE engagement is: understanding what is important to your employees and interacting with them in a way that resonates and aligns with their values and professional goals. Said another way, employee engagement is marketing to the people who are responsible for executing on your strategies and accomplishing your organization's goals. The core purpose of marketing is to establish a reputation (your brand) that attracts and engages customers to support your company, by choosing its products or services over those offered by others. Marketing is not just jargon or advertising, it is everything that communicates with your customers. Successful marketing requires knowing your customers and appealing to them, by using various techniques to reach them. It educates customers about your products or services and plays a key role in the acquisition of customers and generating revenue. Marketing also raises awareness about your brand and what it represents, and engenders customer loyalty. Marketing is tasked with motivating customers to invest their time and money in your company. It is often hard and sometimes impossible to measure the ROI of your marketing efforts. Nevertheless, you know you need to devote resources to marketing and you budget for it, despite the often imperfect, imprecise data available to support the degree of its effectiveness. Marketing to customers is more art than science. Now, reread this paragraph, replacing "customer" with "employee"—that is the function of employee engagement.

Like marketing, employee engagement is essential. Unlike marketing, employee engagement demands full accountability, transparency and no puffery, because it is marketing to employees—the people who are on the inside witnessing everything that happens at the company from a behind-the-scenes viewpoint. Just as companies with great marketing departments become successful by attracting, developing, and retaining ideal customers, companies that "get" employee engagement attract, develop and retain ideal employees. Marketing is costly when it goes wrong or does not work, and the same is true for poor employee engagement. In the United States, Gallup estimates this cost to be more than $300 billion annually just from lost productivity. To successfully engage employees, you as a leader or manager must tap into the hearts, minds, and collective resources of your employees.

Blessing White's 2013 employee engagement report indicates that engagement is lacking in all levels of organizations. The study found that only 59 percent of executives are engaged, which is higher than other employees but still leaves a whopping 41 percent who could benefit from engagement efforts. The study also found that engagement is trickle down, since managers are primarily responsible for employee engagement efforts with programmatic support from HR. These low levels of engagement present significant challenges. Consequences to the companies that participated in the study were eye opening: 31 percent of executives could not innovate effectively, 29 percent were unable pursue attractive market opportunities, and 24 percent had to cancel or delay strategic initiatives.

Just as you invest in marketing to build an emotional connection with your customers, you must invest in employee engagement to connect with your employees in order to grow and secure your market share. Engaged employees provide value to your company not only by doing their job well, but also by contributing more than required, going beyond the scope of their duties to improve processes, attract more customers, and identify cost savings. They go the extra mile to help you succeed because they get an emotional payoff that drives them. And just like customers, the more your employees identify with your core message and purpose, the more loyal they will be to your company and the more likely it is that they will promote your brand to help you attract others to it.

When employees are engaged they bring all of their talents, experience, and connections to work with them. They do not limit their efforts to just the minimum required to do their job or perform their particular role or function. Engagement is the outcome of applying certain principles, taking specific steps to apply them, and using targeted communications designed to inspire, empower, and motivate people to do more. Just like a satisfied customer, whose life is significantly improved by your product and tells everyone she knows about it, engaged employees do not need to be asked to act. They know what needs to be done and they take ownership and offer to help you in whatever way they can. So, for example, an engaged engineering or finance employee will effectively act like a sales or business development representative for your company, becoming a profit center and not just a proverbial cost center.

Gallup recently performed extensive research on employee engagement. It found that the average ratio of engaged to actively disengaged (unhappy, complaining) employees is nearly 2:1. This means the number of employees sabotaging your business is double the number of employees improving your business. Actively disengaged employees erode an organization's productivity and profits in a number of different ways, including poisoning the morale and attitudes of their colleagues in the process. This makes employee engagement a necessary goal for your company if you want to be successful in the marketplace.

Understanding your employees well enough to align your objectives with your employees' personal motivations and values engages their hearts and minds. The result is impactful to your company's bottom line. Engaged employees take ownership, act as marketing channels, and require less managing and oversight. They willingly show up, work long hours, diligently perform their responsibilities, are self-motivated, and voluntarily pitch in to help in any area they can provide assistance to further the company's objectives. Engaged employees cost less to employ: they are healthier (take fewer sick days and have fewer illnesses requiring medical attention), they are more collaborative and productive, they experience fewer interpersonal conflicts and they have higher retention rates. This all results in fewer disgruntled ex-employees and the associated expenditures. Engaged employees attract better talent and more business—customers and clients can tell when they are dealing with a company whose employees are excited and confident about their company's offerings. These good vibes send a subliminal message to customers about the value and trustworthiness of what the company offers. *Engaged employees increase your value.*

Engaged employees will help elevate your company's brand awareness and customer engagement. Now more than ever, customers and clients rely on social proof and find it easily. Social networking is word-of-mouth on steroids. Social proof, or others' experience with a company, has become an integral part of the decision-making process for potential employees, as well as customers. Sites like Glassdoor help establish and perpetuate a company's reputation as an employer. To attract the best employees, you need a sparkling reputation. Now that social media is an essential marketing tool that most employees use personally, it is possible to leverage employees' networks to benefit your business. Opinions and experiences can be shared and "go viral," for better or worse. Engaged employees will be willing to share positively with their networks, while disengaged employees automatically share with the world in a manner that devalues your company.

There are three levels of engagement: *actively engaged* (engaged), *passively disengaged* (neutrally satisfied or apathetic) and *actively disengaged* (saboteur). Actively disengaged employees complain—they raise problems without suggesting solutions; they poison the well and hinder other employees' productivity while deflating morale. They are the least productive, the most likely to take sick days and leaves of absence, and are on the way out either by your choice or theirs. They are also the most likely to sue in the event of a layoff or other reason for discharge. Passively disengaged employees just do their job and collect their pay. They have the greatest potential of becoming actively engaged and studies show they likely constitute more than 50 percent of your employee headcount. Actively engaged employees usually only account for approximately 10 percent of an organization's headcount. It is important to understand these differences in order to target your employee engagement efforts.

Employee engagement is distinct from employee satisfaction, performance, or ambition. Satisfaction and ambition are examples of triggers that may spark emotional commitment and active involvement from an employee that results in better results for your company. Employee performance derives in part from engagement. Employee engagement is the fundamental principle that facilitates attracting great employees and drives excellent employee performance, accomplishment, and retention. It also contributes to continuous organizational improvement all year long, year after year. Essentially it is a reflection of your company's work environment and how the people in your organization interact with each other to drive business results.

So what does employee engagement look like? Employee engagement is present when your employee has an emotional commitment and genuine interest in, and a personal concern for, your organization and its goals. It includes a sense of ownership and pride that is intertwined with their own identity, aligned with personal values and beliefs about their own life purpose as well as their own aspirations in life. Engaged employees actually *care* about their work and their company. They don't work just for a paycheck and benefits, nor view their job as a means to an unrelated end; they work on behalf of the organization's goals as well as their own personal and career development.

Engaged employees display a number of common characteristics and behaviors:

- [ ] Give feedback, good or bad
- [ ] Suggest solutions or strategies to achieve your objectives
- [ ] Do whatever it takes to get the job done
- [ ] Talk about their company with pride
- [ ] Meld their personal identity with their professional persona
- [ ] Ask for additional responsibility or volunteer for projects outside the scope of their responsibilities and otherwise proactively manage their career
- [ ] Recommend or refer others to work for your company
- [ ] Voluntarily step up to act as a leader or take on leadership responsibilities
- [ ] Contribute a positive, can-do attitude and foster teamwork

Accordingly, the engaged computer programmer will help develop the skills of other programmers by answering general questions or providing feedback, even if they are working on different projects. The engaged administrator offers to help people in another department, even when she does not report to them. Another example is the sales person who diligently makes cold calls, even if the boss isn't watching or checking. This means the quality assurance specialist will replace a misbehaving component or address a software bug that needs to be fixed without being asked, even if it's at the end of their day or will mean working through the night. The result: more collaboration, faster completion times and better quality.

Engaged employees lead to better business outcomes. Specifically, Towers Perrin research indicates companies with engaged workers have 6 percent higher net profit margins, and Kenexa research revealed "engaged companies" have five times higher shareholder returns over five years.

The benefits of improving employee engagement throughout your organization are manifold:

✓ Decreased turnover and lower employee acquisition costs

✓ Higher productivity and morale

✓ Greater customer-focus

✓ More creativity and innovation

✓ Improved product and service quality

✓ Greater efficiency and project completion

✓ Increased profits

Collectively, these benefits produce a cascading array of positive outcomes:

✓ Improved customer service, *which leads to...*

✓ Higher customer satisfaction, *which leads to...*

✓ Increased sales (including repeat business and referrals), *which leads to...*

✓ Higher levels of revenue and profit, *which leads to...*

✓ Higher shareholder returns and higher stock prices, *which leads to...*

✓ *A Sustainable Future Proof Company.*

Former Campbell's Soup CEO, Doug Conant, succinctly summed up why employee engagement is worth investing in when he said, "To win in the marketplace you must first win in the workplace."

"To win in the marketplace you must first win in the workplace."

Fortunately, improving employee engagement isn't rocket science; planning for engagement is formulaic and can be tailored to the particular needs and budget of your organization. However, it must be ingrained in your company's culture to successfully motivate your employees to consistently make valuable contributions and strive to help your company achieve its goals. Employee engagement is a habit, not a corporate initiative nor just the job of Human Resources or assignment for managers to do once (or even a few times a year). It is more than a policy or initiative—it is a context, an all-pervasive, ever-present environment. That culture will prove conducive to productivity, collaboration, creativity, innovation, safety, quality, excellence, accountability, stewardship, and goal achievement.

Employee engagement must be a company-wide responsibility, to be effective and beneficial. Engagement research underscores this with findings that employees' perceptions of their primary manager influence about 70 percent of their engagement. Meanwhile coworkers' attitudes and other environmental factors account for the remaining 30 percent. Hewlett-Packard co-founder David Packard said, "Marketing is too important to be left to the marketing department." Those are wise and true words that apply to employee engagement. Employee engagement is not just an issue for the HR department to manage. It takes consistent and constant effort, skill, and multiple "touches" to engage employees and customers alike, because people are busier than ever before. Employee engagement is focused on the human factors, on which every person on a team has an impact.

Think of employee engagement as the pistons in your car engine, an integral component without which the engine cannot work. No engine, no propulsion, no forward motion. Now imagine that your company is that car and your employee engagement level is running its engine. You don't want a clunker; you want a Tesla Roadster! You need a high-performance engine capable of enabling your roadster to take you where you want to go—quickly and efficiently. The following chapters will show you which components need to be tuned for optimal road worthiness and exactly how to make those tweaks to take your organization's performance from mild to wild!

Chapter 2

THE WHEELS OF ENGAGEMENT

Communication And Diversity Steer The Direction Of Employees' Focus

Diversity: the art of thinking independently together.

—MALCOLM FORBES

WHAT DOES DIVERSITY HAVE to do with employee engagement? In a word: Everything. People are inherently diverse in age, ethnic origin, education, economic background, and as many more categories as you can imagine. The workforce is more ethnically and generationally diverse than ever before, which comes with benefits as well as challenges. In order to capture the attention, maximize the time, and obtain the best efforts of all the different people in your organization, it is essential that you appeal to these diversity factors. It is essential to have dissimilarities in your organization, as well as identifying and addressing the inherent biases and other complications that such diversity presents. To develop a culture that incorporates and leverages diversity, it helps to really understand why you want it. Diversity for diversity's sake (to achieve some preconceived statistical pie chart) is not effective;

however, diversifying your team is like diversifying your investment portfolio—it provides safety and an assured upside over time. Gaining the benefits of diversity results from authentically adopting a mindset that celebrates and honors different opinions, styles, interests, and proficiencies.

BENEFITS OF DIVERSITY

While people of similar background and life experience share certain values or opinions and tend to congregate naturally, connecting people from different walks of life yields synergies that help formulate superior strategies, solutions, and products. In this global and increasingly competitive economy, where talent is crucial to improving your bottom line, it is imperative that you apply marketing principles to the discovery of the most beneficial ways of building and developing your team, to maximize your returns. Attracting the largest and most diverse set of candidates and retaining your best performers is increasingly necessary to engage employees and customers in the near and long term.

Increasing diversity will improve your company's market share. In 2011, Deloitte conducted a quantitative study[1] that revealed astounding growth in the buying power of various ethnic minority groups between 1990 and 2014. Each of these group's market influence and buying clout exceeded that of Caucasians by 2014. A McKinsey study on gender diversity and company performance found that on average, Fortune 500 companies with the highest percentages of female corporate officers reported a 35.1 percent higher return on equity and a 34 percent higher return to shareholders over companies with the lowest percentages of females in these corporate management slots. Moreover, according to the US Census Bureau, by 2043, no single racial or ethnic group will constitute a majority of the population. This trend exists in many other geographical regions as well. Your employees need to mirror and share your customers' affinities and values if your company is to serve your customers well enough to keep them and attract new ones. As a business leader, leveraging diversity is the most effective response you can have to the changing market. Ensuring diversity throughout your workforce will culti-vate broader thinking and enable your organization to identify and capture opportunities it might otherwise miss.

A diverse organization brings together a balanced mix of people from dif-ferent ethnic and socioeconomic backgrounds which leads to more creative and productive teams at all levels. The more successful you are at attracting a diverse pool of candidates, the more likely you are to hire the brightest and best for every team within your organization. Having an inclusive, discrimi-nation-free work environment enables you to retain these individuals, as well as existing employees who possess deep knowledge and already understand the inner workings of your organization. By reducing expenses associated with attrition and disgruntled employees, this approach will not only save your company money, it will actually boost revenues and profits. Bringing together people with different qualifications and perspectives ensures that your team will be poised to problem-solve and deliver excellent solutions that foster innovation, keeping your company relevant and competitive in the marketplace.

To realize the performance benefits of diversity, you will need to reach beyond token measures in integrating people of various races, ethnicities, religions, and gender preferences in every department and level of your company. A company culture that incorporates *all* kinds of diversity (not just legally recognized classifications) *at all levels* is key to growing and sus-taining a strong and engaged team that will drive your company's economy for the long haul: women and men from a variety of ethnic and economic backgrounds should be well represented in your C-suite and boardroom, as well as the rest of your company. According to Deloitte, corporate boards and senior management of Fortune 500 companies currently only include 14.5 percent and 18 percent of people of color and women respectively. Hiring ex-ecutives with a breadth of experience and perspectives that map your market more closely will make your company stronger. Recruiting efforts focused on promoting diversity is just a small piece of the engagement mosaic, however.

Building a reputation for accommodating and respecting differences of all kinds will facilitate efforts to reach out to a diverse talent pool to find qualified people who are really passionate about your company. Further, the steps your organization takes to build a reputation as diversity-friendly workplace will also promote great employee morale, while boosting performance and increasing retention.. For example, embracing unorthodox methods of identifying opportunities for employees to expand their skills and develop expertise, as well as creating more ways to advance employees' careers, has proven to be a highly successful tactic for developing engagement. Many of the established and growing companies listed in Forbes' "The Best Companies To Work For In 2014" enable employees to design new jobs for themselves, schedule flexible work hours, and take advantage of training and other professional development opportunities. The benefits you offer will promote diversity if they transcend differences to be broadly applicable and meaningful to all of your employees, regardless of life circumstances, experience level, and professional discipline. People tend to gossip about the perks their employer offers, and that's a great back-channel approach to getting your employees to voluntarily raise brand awareness and promote your company.

Integrating diversity into policies, programs, benefits, training, and everyday activities shows employees you care about them; it facilitates alignment of interests. Diversity requires training programs to ensure the development of clear and respectful communication by encouraging sensitivity to biases, stereotypes, and cultural or generational differences among employees. These programs more than pay for themselves in savings from reduced turnover and litigation, as well as increased productivity and revenue. The aforementioned 2013 Gallup study found that hiring a demographically diverse workforce can improve a company's financial performance. That study of more than 800 businesses also found that in particular, gender-diverse business units have 14–18 percent better financial outcomes than those dominated by one gender. When gender-diverse teams are also highly engaged, revenues register a 46–58 percent boost. The different approaches and viewpoints brought to the table when men and women work together in balanced proportions yields better problem solving as well as more ideas and solutions. Additionally, the more your team's makeup reflects society, the greater likelihood employees will stay engaged.

As used in this book, "diversity" is broadly defined to include many facets of differences beyond race and gender. In the context of the workplace, diversity manifests itself in age, personality types, physical attributes, sexual orientation, educational background, income, marital status, geographical location, spiritual practice, parental status, work experience, and job function. Successful employee engagement requires that people with different backgrounds, interests, priorities, and opinions work together as a team to accomplish things that a homogenous group could not produce. Fostering a corporate culture that emphasizes communication and teamwork among the diverse population is the best path to effective collaboration and your organization's success. Your diversity efforts should not be structured as stand-alone programs or driven by a single department; rather, they should be hardwired into your organization's DNA and implemented throughout your company. When diversity is part and parcel of your corporate culture, marketers will gladly capitalize on it.

Diversity and engagement work together to improve efficiency and performance. They are both cultural elements, and they shape your organization's performance much as the contours of an automobile's body affect its performance on the road. Acceptance, curiosity, and respect should be nurtured in your organizational culture to advance and sustain diversity and engagement. Though rarely addressed, one of the reasons diversity and engagement efforts fall short is the impact of inherent biases. Every human has biases, some of which are consciously chosen or at least identified, while others are unrecognized and subconscious. People can control and manage their conscious biases, but latent biases also come out in communications, decisions, and actions and often have unintended consequences. This is how breakdowns occur. Elimination of bias through diversity and communication training can raise awareness, highlight similarities amongst differences, and provide tools to help people manage conflicts and work together in a more collaborative manner. For engagement and diversity to work their magic on team performance, these barriers and obstacles to your team's success must be identified and addressed.

As humans, we all have automatic, hardwired preferences and perspectives that color our perceptions and drive reactions. These unconscious autopilot behaviors are the hidden biases that exist within every member of your team and are at the core of miscommunications, conflicts, and working styles. To improve the way different individuals work together, these hidden biases must be uncovered. Once revealed, such differences can be managed and leveraged. Biases are also inherent in organizational structures, so it is important to identify those as well. A complimentary Corporate Diversity Assessment, as well as a Diversity Self Assessment, is available to you by visiting www.employeeandclientengagement.com/contact/. This brief assessment will help you identify areas within your company where diversity can be improved, and provides a tool to fine-tune communications and further engage your team.

In business as in society, there are countless examples of groups of individuals coming together based on shared connections of all types: cultural, ethnic, religious, gender, interest, experience, age, and/or sexual orientation-based. There are benefits to that, including positioning your workplace as a positive shared experience. There is extraordinary value in welcoming and encouraging different types of people to contribute to achieving your goals. Company-wide practices that include targeted two-way communication, assessment, action, and feedback should be implemented and consistently followed to successfully extract and optimize the value created by the unique blend of people on your team. Think of diversity and engagement as power additives that will rev up your organization's engine.

In marketing, prospective customers are analyzed and categorized based on their demographics and psychographics to help determine what messaging and delivery mediums will best appeal to them. Employees, like customers span a wide array of demographics and psychographics, so a variety of messages and communication techniques are needed to direct and focus their efforts. Using the demographic, and especially psychographic, information you already have about your employees, you can align each of their respective needs and talents with your organization's objectives. The result will be a more energized, committed, and focused team.

To hire and sustainably motivate high-performing team members with varied backgrounds, you must also recognize and acknowledge that non -traditional work arrangements, flexible structures and a clear career path are attractive incentives for today's diverse talent. This ensures integration and guards against the "diversity without inclusion" trap. A symptom of this pothole is failing to engage and retain diverse talent. For example, many high-performing women leave companies after having kids because their advancement opportunities become limited or other barriers to their success become apparent. Another sign of a deficiency and room for improvement is when certain ethnic groups or genders are underrepresented in specific functional groups. When a diverse mix of people do not work well together, some people feel left out or discriminated against. When this occurs, differences between people are not the problem. The issue is how the people are communicating with each other and how the team is managed. It is also a clue that diversity is not seamlessly woven into the culture of your organization.

A holistic approach to engagement and diversity will move the needle towards noticeably positive results. Interpersonal conflicts often arise when communication falters or diversity is mismanaged, resulting in lost productivity, diminished morale, and employee turnover (usually it's the best people who jump ship), ultimately hurting your bottom line. Inclusion necessitates a coordinated approach that involves employees at all levels and in all functions. The following chart outlines ways to engage an entire company in diversity efforts.

Leadership accountability	Set goals for all functional groups	Align diversity goals with corporate goals	Incorporate diversity into your culture and reputation
Include diversity goals in executive compensation for all executives as well as managers in all functions.	Incorporate diversity goals into performance evaluations for all employees.	Create a diversity strategy that supports the corporate mission.	Build diversity into corporate communications, employee benefits and programs, recruiting, organizational changes, succession planning and marketing.
Include people development budgets and goals around diversifying talent and teams.	Have every functional group set diversity goals for its organization and identify specifically how its function will contribute to a more inclusive workplace. Require all functional groups to select some percentage of vendor spend on companies owned by minorities and women.	Determine how diversity will contribute to your business growth.	Establish a record of external recognition from organizations such as: Diversity, Inc.; Catalyst; Working Mother magazine; the Human Rights Campaign; Forbes, etc.
Develop processes and metrics for accountability in recruiting, retention, development, advancement, bottom-line impact, etc.		Establish diversity councils throughout the organization to empower all employees to innovate, provide feedback, and implement changes.	Develop relationships with women and minority leadership organizations; select related philanthropies to support.

Communications are a fundamental element of engagement; they can make or break inclusion. Whether you are appealing to potential customers or engaging team members in your vision and goals, your desired outcome is a specific action and level of participation. Just as marketing messaging is designed to engage particular customers, your communications with employees should consider their viewpoints and needs. Communications with your employees need to be tailored to relate to a variety of individuals to motivate teams and organizations comprised of people from diverse backgrounds or disciplines. For example, some people prefer face-to-face interaction, while others like email, and still others prefer voice (phone), texting, or some form of instant messaging. As a manager, it is best to find out how members of your team like to communicate, and converse with them accordingly. Small adjustments like this can have a huge impact in the quality of your personal interactions with employees, while improving the attitude and productivity of your team.

Employees will respond better to internal communications if they are delivered using a variety of media with tailored messaging (e.g. particular groups or functions, translating to other languages, or incorporating catchphrases and examples). Additionally, incorporate examples of workplace inclusion in your team and corporate communications by adding quotes about diversity and inserting excerpts from a variety of sources to newsletters, announcements, and email signatures. Invite your employees to submit their favorite diversity-related news articles, statistics, or quotes and use them in internal materials as well as those targeted to customers. Think about using these submissions in your social media posts to demonstrate your attention to diversity. Diversity materials can also be used as meeting icebreakers or during teambuilding activities. You can use this same type of activity to promote deeper conversations about diversity in your organization among leadership teams and committees.

Leverage diversity to brainstorm new ideas and facilitate change. Everyone on your team—even those who seem so much like you—has a unique perspective and blend of skills, interests, and motivations. To inspire them to go the extra mile and invest their passion and full energy towards helping you achieve your objectives, it is necessary to make connections between them as individuals and their respective roles on your team. This requires ongoing, skilled, and sometimes difficult conversations. Most people either shy away from challenging communications because they perceive them to be confrontational, or because they simply do not have the skills to smoothly navigate the twists and turns of discussions that may be charged with emotion. Additionally, communication styles differ widely amongst diverse individuals. Communications workshops are excellent professional development tools to improve these skills, develop managers and enhance employee performance. Furthermore, incorporating these types of workshops into teambuilding activities provides an opportunity to better understand what motivates and drives your employees. Trainings that boost communication skills and facilitate respecting differences, demonstrate that you are concerned about your employees' overall well-being, while ensuring the health of your organization.

A surefire way to foster respect and diversity is to model and incorporate the following basics into your diversity efforts:

- ☐ If a coworker or employee has a name that's difficult to pronounce, make a concentrated effort to say the person's name correctly. You can also ask your employee to say his name for you, listen carefully, and repeat it back until you get it.

- ☐ On the other hand, avoid giving employees nicknames—that is alienating. If you really cannot pronounce a name after giving it your best effort, then ask your colleague if there is some other way she likes to be addressed.

- ☐ Avoid promulgating stereotypes and spouting racial, religious, and gender jokes. Such behavior is alienating and makes people uncomfortable, thus breeding divisiveness. Why would you want to risk this?

- ☐ Learn about various cultural holidays and traditions. Diverse environments give you an opportunity to explore the world right where you sit; potlucks and celebrations of colleagues' respective festivals are fun and show interest and respect. Your employees will be happy to share this information with you and a more open line of communication will be created. Additionally, think of this as a practice that promotes the profoundly powerful trait of empathy.

- ☐ Help employees identify the similarities amongst each other. This will facilitate a healthy working environment and culture of inclusion.

- ☐ Keep the "human aspect" in mind. Every person has a personal life and it is important to respect and value that by not encroaching on this important component of well-being.

- ☐ Manage the perceptual, cultural, and language barriers related to diversity to ensure they don't give way to confusion and low team spirit.

☐ Include diverse groups of employees in all strategic decisions. Collecting opinions from a diverse group of people can change the way business is done for the better. A person from a different background may offer a perspective on an issue that no one else has given. This not only increases innovation and quality, it engages employees by imparting a sense of ownership while establishing trust.

Here are a few additional steps for you to consider:

☐ **Committing resources to recruiting minorities** on college campuses and at job fairs, conferences, and in appropriate publications.

☐ **Retaining and promoting minority employees** by providing coaching, formal mentoring, training, and leadership-development programs aimed at helping them advance their careers.

☐ **Providing diversity information** on your company websites, mission statements, policies, annual reports, videos, recruitment literature, and advertisements.

☐ **Promoting diversity** in managerial and leading positions.

☐ **Arranging training and assistance** that improve policies and procedures related to diversity.

Creating a diversity-friendly culture is about making sure everyone feels valued. In turn, the value of your organization will rise. Diverse teams can contribute more, with higher quality and greater relevance to today's market. Investments in promoting and sustaining diversity will pay rich dividends through increased employee and customer engagement and increased revenues. Of course, diversity alone will not deliver on the promise of engagement and all its upsides. Members of a team not only need to respect and trust each other, they must also understand how they, individually, fit into the big picture and how to work with their colleagues to drive in the same direction. Chapter 3 provides guidance and tips that will help you improve teamwork.

Chapter 3

MORE THAN ONE DRIVER

Engagement Roles And Responsibilities

*According to legend, when asked what he was doing, a janitor at
NASA replied "I'm helping to put a man on the Moon."*

DO YOU WANT EVERYONE on your team contributing 100 percent of their
ability towards achieving your organizations goals? Do you want to work
with people who enjoy what they do and contribute more than required? Do
you want employees who you can count on to do whatever it takes to achieve
project milestones? Imagine what it would feel like in your company, and
look like in your financials, if teams were enthusiastic, cooperative, focused,
productive, and loyal. Hiring employees who have a "can-do" attitude and
possess basic people skills, as well as the required technical qualifications, is
a step in the right direction. However, even the best candidates will fall short
of being ideal employees unless they are set up for success—which begs the
question: Who is responsible for creating an environment that breed success
for your company as well as employees? The answer: everyone at all levels in
your organization. Executives, managers, HR, and the individual employees
themselves, all have a role to play in engagement.

Borrowing from marketing terminology, there are two types of engagement: *push* and *pull.* Both types are necessary to successfully sustain a culture that inspires employees to care about their company. Push engagement is employer driven. This is when your company provides benefits and work arrangements and other conditions designed to entice, retain, and delight employees to encourage them to devote more time and effort at work. Pull engagement is employee driven and includes mentoring, resource groups, and committees of employees that drive initiatives and special projects. Pull engagement motivates employees to take a personal interest in how they impact the company's outcomes. This ties your company's success directly to their efforts and gives your team a true sense of ownership. Pull engagement depends on some level of push engagement. Basically, employees will invest in you by taking positive actions to further your organization's reputation and interests *if you invest in them.* Engagement is an interaction based upon mutual benefit, respect, and collaboration.

What are the key roles and responsibilities that produce employee engagement? Executives set the vision, mission, and overall strategy for a company, but they also craft the tone and culture in a variety of ways including determinations regarding where to devote greater resources. Engagement initiatives require executive buy-in and long-term commitment to derive the most benefit; HR's role is largely reliant on executive direction. Ideally, HR develops an overall engagement strategy, policies to support it and advises executives and managers at all levels in its execution. Managers have a direct and immediate impact on employee engagement. Ultimately, employees determine their own level of engagement. How many times have you seen a revolving door in certain departments of a company that otherwise has a history of stable staffing? It is common to hear employees rave or complain about their job based solely on their experience with *their* manager. So you should be training your managers in a variety of soft skills to nurture employee engagement.

Great managers engage their teams on several levels. From the beginning, they display genuine care and concern for their people. Building on that basic human connection, a superb manager will develop strong, trusting relationships with her staff, engendering an open and positive work atmosphere in which employees feel supported and respected. Allow, indeed encourage, yourself to care just as much about your people as individuals as you care about their performance. This sets the stage for high performance by enabling you to identify how you can structure your team members to contribute based on their respective strengths and interests. This also paves the way for you to identify paths to individually motivate your employees to work and strive harder. Finally, it is necessary to invest in developing your employees' professional skills to set them up for success and advancement. This benefits your organization by boosting productivity, innovation, and retention. Additionally, invest in your own development—especially in ways that foster a talent for supporting, positioning, empowering, and engaging your staff.

Aligning the mission, needs, and spirit of your organization with the interests, experience, and temperament of your employees is an ongoing process, not just a factor in hiring decisions. Although full alignment may exist, or *seem* to exist, at one point in time, it is subject to change. Like cars, relationships become misaligned and must be realigned as part of their routine maintenance. Establishing and maintaining open lines of communication with your employees is the most reliable way of achieving this. The quality of those connections determines your degree of success in leading and managing your employees. Trust is the key to maximizing the input and information shared between employees and management at all levels. And trust, like communication, is a two-way street.

How do you trust when the stakes are high? That question is ever-present in everyone's mind—the stakes are high for every member of your team, as well as for you and your organization. That is where a degree of alignment between management, individual employees, and the company's objectives always exists. Building from an understanding of this interdependence, teams can line up and forge ahead with optimal efficiency to reach any target. When employees trust you, they will give you reliable information and more constructive input. When you trust your employees, you empower them to step out and up to contribute more and provide greater value. Synergies start to form and the impossible becomes possible as the team consistently rises to overcome challenges. It takes effort, attention, and diligence to achieve this, but the payoff is worth the investment, yes?

According to various studies on the results of actively engaging employees, payoffs include greater commitment, productivity, and higher profits. A recent Gallup survey revealed the shocking truth that the vast majority of employees worldwide report an overall negative experience at work. Barely more than one in ten employees indicate feeling involved in and enthusiastic about their jobs and committed to their organization's success. On the flip side, organizations with loyal and dedicated employees were shown to out -perform those with low commitment scores by 47 percent in a 2000 study and by 200 percent in the 2002 follow-on study by the consulting firm of Watson Wyatt (now Towers Watson). According to a more recent report in the *Industrial and Labor Relations Review* (2012), employees with the highest levels of commitment (using the same definition as "engagement" in this book) perform 20 percent better and are 87 percent less likely to leave an organization. And a study of professional service firms revealed that offices with engaged employees were up to 43 percent more productive than offices with neutral or disengaged employees. But according to Gallup's 2012 survey of companies worldwide, only 3 percent of employees are actively engaged in their jobs, while 63 percent may be satisfied or neutral (and are not engaged) and 24 percent are actively disengaged. The same survey also showed that for the company to realize significant profit benefits, the majority of employees at a company need to be engaged.. Conversely, companies with the highest engagement scores had 10 percent higher customer ratings, 21 percent higher productivity, 25–65 percent less turnover, 41 percent higher quality and safety, 37 percent less absenteeism and were 22 percent more profitable.

Bottom line: employees are the number one priority, alongside customers, for the success of your company.

Therefore it is wise to invest in engaging your employees to the same degree you invest in marketing to your customers. Management's communication skills are central to engagement. To drive alignment that spurs high performance, it is key to communicate through a variety of modes, both formal and informal. Feedback, information exchanges, suggestions, observations, reviews, teambuilding activities, facilitated brainstorming and strategy sessions, as well as professional development and training, are all crucial components of alignment and overall engagement efforts. Just as your company has a marketing strategy based on key principles, alignment is a cornerstone of any employee engagement strategy. A coordinated effort between executives, HR, and managers is needed to ensure policies and corporate messaging to employees are consistent with goal setting and other information managers share with employees and receive from employees. Clarity is essential to align and engage employees.

Candid, frequent conversations with team members shed light on misunderstandings and other issues before they become roadblocks or worse. Job expectations, responsibilities, goals, and performance evaluations must be clear, and appropriate support should be provided to help employees drive and accelerate results. In order to ensure your team has everything it needs to succeed, it is important to listen to employees' feedback and take responsive actions that demonstrate you are actively *listening* and heard what they said. Integrating proven best practices, like weekly 1:1s and regular team meetings, with modern stylings, such as walking meetings and group meals, creates settings that are more conducive to generating quality conversations. Transparency, consistency, and supportive action engender trust, facilitate understanding, and keep efforts focused and free of petty distractions. In other words, the core of keeping your team aligned comes down to following this simple rule: Listen, Say what you mean, Do what you say you will do, and don't be mean."

Observing that simple tenet, combined with welcoming and incorporating suggestions for improvements, opens the door to employees taking ownership of whole areas of responsibility. While it is important for everyone on your team to have some defined responsibility—a role that everyone knows a particular person can be counted on to fulfill—flexibility is equally important. Providing regular opportunities for your team members to redefine or expand their talents, interests and roles in a way that better aligns with your company's objectives is an easy win-win. Facilitated brainstorming sessions are a powerful tool to solicit ideas and arrive at solutions with assigned owners and accountability, in an efficient way that ensures everyone is on the same page. The role of the facilitator is to manage time, keep the discussion on track, take notes, and be sure everyone is heard—as well as contributing observations where appropriate and providing an organized summary. Failing to seek out and adopt recommendations from your colleagues sends a message that you view them as cogs in a wheel, which leads to demoralizing and limiting beliefs and statements like "I'm just doing my job" and "That's not my job, that's so and so's job."

When employees are focused on just doing their job and keeping their paycheck, they are disengaged and misaligned. Your "high potentials" will not stay if they feel they are inhibited from contributing the most value, or undermined by others' lack of effort; they often become disengaged and exit when they see pervasive low morale or no path for recognition and advancement. Distractions caused by co-worker conflicts, corporate intrigue resulting from lack of transparency or clarity, and lack of necessary resources, undermine engagement and productivity. Having periodic, candid communications with your employees to connect the dots between what they are working on and the company's mission, as well as progress towards immediate goals, promotes alignment. When your employees' values naturally coincide with your organization's mission, helping them see the link between their daily tasks and the big picture keeps them engaged. The better they understand their piece of the puzzle, the more effectively they can help you achieve your goals and feel more invested in them.

Frequent and honest feedback is the simplest way to support your employees' goals, as well as your own. The most effective performance feedback is given daily, in informal ways—this could be a simple acknowledgement or comment in an e-mail or impromptu conversation. Leveraging your weekly 1:1s to provide guidance, ask questions, and recognize victories as well as mistakes (large and small), will keep your team on track and eliminate surprises in annual performance reviews. It is imperative to acknowledge excellent performance as well as areas for improvement, stating plainly what is expected. Be specific and encourage actions you want to see and reinforce behaviors you want your employee to repeat. Of course, these communications should be respectful and neutral, showing enthusiastic praise and empathetic constructive criticism. When you give feedback, strive to tie it to your employee's individual goals as well as those of the organization.

When you—as an executive, leader, and manager—grease the engagement wheel, employees will have a greater opportunity to commit their "discretionary effort" and skills to performing at their highest level in alignment with your objectives. Still, employees must be coached in the art of directing their own careers. It is important for each member of your team to understand the role they play in their own development and success. Employees must engage themselves; ultimately, it is their choice. Providing a resource or ongoing program to foster and assist ambitious employees goes a long way towards make managers' jobs easier and boosting morale. Even most experienced employees simply do not know how to take charge of their careers or perhaps they have cultural or generational values that get in the way. Junior employees in particular often fail to actively manage their advancement for a variety of reasons. Your communications and organizational culture can invite employees to take initiative—or inadvertently discourage and squelch that possibility.

The truest proof of engagement is visible in the interactions and results your organization generates. When everyone is involved in a coordinated effort to ensure that ownership and initiative are core values that are consistently reflected in everyday actions and communications, growth and sustainability is assured. On the other hand, disengagement is equally obvious in the consequences and challenges your company faces. You know engagement when you see it: high performing employees aligned with your mission and driving together in a direction that makes your vision a reality. People power the engine that drives your company, so it is important to understand their motivations, concerns, attitudes, values, beliefs, and other qualities that affect their behavior under all circumstances. Chapter 4 explores these elements, across the four generations in today's workplace.

Chapter 4

PEOPLE ARE THE ENGINE

Sparking The Pistons Of Each Generation

We open up a quarrel
Between the present and the past
We only sacrifice the future
[We] may have a new perspective
On a different day

B. A. Robertson (of Mike & the Mechanics),
"The Living Years"

OUR MODERN WORKPLACE IS unique in the span of generations working side by side. With so many different views on the nature of "work," it's no wonder there are complaints, conflicts, and communication breakdowns. Unfortunately, if those challenges are not addressed head-on, morale and productivity suffer and the profitability of your company takes a big hit.

Companies that have been in existence for more than fifty years have dealt with executive succession at least once, along with the numerous transitions of managers and individual contributors passing the baton from one generation to the next. This generational changing of the guard was relatively straightforward when people stayed with one company throughout most of their career. Even when that changed, there were still no more than two or three generations working together and they generally agreed on their respective places in an organization. But the days when professional roles were based on experience and age are gone. Modern succession planning is much more complicated, and newer companies cannot rely on the "proven" methods that were previously employed by such companies as IBM, Xerox, and Procter & Gamble. You and your team face a number of challenges in assigning employees to appropriate roles.

While certain motivational approaches are timeless (generous compensation packages and promotion or award structures, for example), new solutions are needed as your staff becomes more diverse. Your generational beliefs and biases may be thwarting your efforts to make necessary changes to retain your most talented and accomplished employees. The trusted succession planning strategies that previously worked for blue chip companies, when the workforce was much more homogeneous, simply do not work well today and will not work at all in the future. This offers an opportunity for you to try out new ideas, knowing that you are in a pioneering era that demands and welcomes change. It also presents the possibility of being viewed as a trendsetter in your industry, as you create novel best practices to head off the common problem of dismal employee engagement. Possessing that coveted status will not only help your organization hire and retain the best employees, it will boost financial performance.

To ensure the success of your company, you need to foster a multigenerational handshake on mutual respect, communication and collaboration. Successfully managing multigenerational teams is crucial to the performance of your company, regardless of its size, industry, or market share. If you are a baby boomer or Gen Xer, you must respect and embrace millennials and mentor them. If you are a millennial, seize the opportunity to tap into the strengths and wisdom offered by your boomer and Xer peers. Today's young business executives are tomorrow's senior business leaders; they'll need to know how to manage teams with different ideas about how things should be done and history holds lessons.

As you know, Gen X and Gen Y employees are restless; typically, they do not stay with one employer for more than a few years. Women are still woefully underrepresented in technology companies despite the expanded female technology candidate pool from Gens X and Y. This is largely because of attitudes and other cultural factors that lead women of all ages to feel unwelcome, underestimated, and undervalued. Further, many high performing women leave the workforce at the peak of their careers in favor of entrepreneurial or other pursuits that afford them more flexibility to care for their families. With regard to working women, the convergence of generational and gender issues will significantly impact your organization if it has not already. Fifty percent of the working population in the US is now made up of women, and women account for more than 50 percent of the consumer market. Accordingly, the success of your company depends on its ability to attract and retain highly qualified female employees.

Successfully managing multigenerational teams begins with understanding what makes the members of each generation tick. This includes their values, influences, and perspectives, as well as their experiences, work ethic, and worldview. We'll consider all of those elements and more as they relate to the "traditionalists," the baby boomers, and representatives of Gens X and Y. You'll want to share these insights with managers and your team, to improve communications. People interact more positively when they have an appreciation for others' experiences, because that understanding eliminates confusion and neutralizes the stories people conjure. Having a basic sense of where your colleagues are coming from will help you and your team be more tolerant and open to each others different perspectives. Also, synergies become possible when you and everyone on your team are empowered to openly share your thoughts and be heard. With this foundation, your staff will become inclined to ask questions before jumping to conclusions based on stereotypes and assumptions.

Since we're all human, it's helpful to assume there are some common values and views all your employees share. The key is to identify the intersections of agreement among your generationally diverse teams and prospective employees. For example, regardless of age, your team members will align behind doing something to deliver "quality results that provide value." This particular message speaks to the core values of people born after 1940 through the present, including Generation Z who will start to enter the workforce within the next few years. While each generation perceives some things differently—choosing to emphasize certain qualities and deemphasize others—common themes can be detected. It is incumbent upon you to ensure your people and organizational structures bridge the generation gaps.

"You will find that most employees will be happy to attend training for this purpose: "do the work to grow personally in order to get better results and contribute more to the world."

Fortunately there is a theme you can leverage to link generations and capture their collective interest: personal and professional development courses. You will find that most employees will be happy to attend training for this purpose: "do the work to grow personally in order to get better results and contribute more to the world." Communication is the key to bringing together a broad range of generation-specific perspectives and experiences for problem solving. While the words and phrases different people use to express themselves may vary, resulting in misinterpretation and frustration, the intentions are frequently remarkably similar. As with foreign languages, the words each generation uses can be translated to reveal the underlying meaning. As marketing attempts to influence people by getting into their world and appealing to their desires, your interactions with employees, and

---

their interactions with their fellow workers, will either foster engagement or undermine it.

It is said that you cannot understand a person until you walk a mile in their shoes. To get into the respective worlds of your company's generationally diverse population, you need to gain a sense of what it is like to experience their world through their eyes. Listed below are some of the core drivers of each generation mentioned (with the caveat that these are generally held beliefs). This information, along with the year ranges ascribed to each generation, is based on extensive research undertaken and compiled by the West Midland Family Center, a nonprofit devoted to intergenerational issues:

Traditionalists (1900–45)

✓ Work hard and rewards will come later; humility

✓ Follow the rules in order to contribute to the collective good

✓ Giving back is important

✓ Don't question authority; show respect, deference

✓ Loyalty and family focused

✓ Take responsibility (translation: personal accountability and self-sufficiency)

Baby Boomers (1946–64)

✓ Equality

✓ Loyal to children

✓ Personal gratification and growth

✓ Desire to make a difference

✓ Questioners/suspicious

Gen X (1965–80)

✓ Pragmatic, informal, and self-reliant

✓ Big thinkers

✓ Technology literate

✓ Work–life balance and strong desire for fun

Millennials (1981–2000)

✓ Diversity and highly tolerant

✓ Achievement, fun, and competition orientated

✓ Tech savvy, highly educated and highly sociable

✓ Self-confident; like attention

✓ Avid consumers with high morals

Gen Z (approximately late 1990s–present, according to Sparks and Honey marketing agency's study)

✓ Largest generational group on the US

✓ Desire change

✓ Formal (school) education less important

✓ Multitaskers, always connected digitally

✓ Independent/self-sufficient (partially because of worry about the economy)

✓ Distrust corporations and large institutions

The key areas of the differences at play between these generations in the work setting are: technology, work ethic or perspective on work- life balance, relationships, view of authority, outlook on the future, view of money, leadership style, and communication style.

As a group, millennials are the employees who are most experienced and comfortable with technology. They see technology as being ubiquitous and not only helpful, but necessary. Because this generation is so well educated and sees ways to contribute efficiencies, there is an expectation that their employer will value and respect them from Day One, regardless of titles, position, and years of experience (or lack of same). Since their opinions were solicited and honored as children, Millennials have a relaxed attitude toward authority. As adults, they see themselves as being just as capable as any other adult and want to be treated accordingly. Nonetheless, this group wants to continuously learn and be challenged, and makes a habit of collaboration. These employees expect instant and frequent (preferably positive/constructive) feedback, as that is what they are accustomed to from their upbringing. They are conditioned and internally driven to achieve (the key is to find out what each individual wants to achieve, to ensure that is aligned with your objectives and needs). On the flip-side, they tend to expect success to come easily and quickly.

Millennial team members appreciate mentors who offer growth and development opportunities with a clear set of expectations and a structured outline of goals and steps to achieve them. Flexibility and time for fun and creativity are extremely important, as is socializing with colleagues at work. Money is viewed primarily as a reward for doing meaningful work, and meaningful work that meshes with the individual's desired lifestyle is a requirement. Money is important, but only to the extent it is needed and it is not valued to the degree previous generations valued it. The total work environment is a factor the millennial generation evaluates and weights heavily in making job decisions.

Gen X is also typically highly educated and experienced, and its members do not automatically respect authority. This group grew up in a changing world, when equal rights for minorities and women were hot issues. Accordingly, they tend to be more open to change and do not have a hierarchical mindset towards people. This generation witnessed authority figures, such as governmental officials and corporate moguls, lie and make embarrassing and costly mistakes that caused economic crises. Many of these people were raised by single or divorced parents, or in homes where both parents worked. They became self-sufficient at a young age; the term "latch-key kid" was coined for them. As a result of their environmental influences, your Gen X team members and managers are concerned with work–life balance, have high expectations and a default attitude of distrust.

This group of individuals comprises skilled problem-solvers who thrive on guidelines and hands-off management, appreciate direct communication, and work efficiently. Also known as "the doer generation," they are proactive, eager to learn, and determined to develop their skills. They are very malleable and adapt well to change. They view technology as a helpful tool (when it works). Stagnation is boring and doing things that are wasteful or for no apparent reason kills their motivation. Money is important to these workers, as they are the first generation in the US whose members are collectively less well off than their parents. Many Gen Xers are caregivers to both children and parents by virtue of becoming parents later in life, combined with the fact that their parents are living longer. Flexibility is highly valued and time off is a desirable reward, as work is often viewed as a means to an end. That said, this generation is results-oriented and its constituents seek, from their staff and themselves, to "get it done" and move on to the next thing.

Baby boomers value collaboration and ambition, and appreciate others who work hard. Appearances and status matter a great deal to this demographic. Money is linked to status, a vestigial artifact of the "American dream" they were raised to believe in. Based on their experience "paying their dues" and their intense focus on professional achievement, they expect productive employees to work long hours and want younger colleagues to respect them.

For this group, the work environment was unforgiving and rigid; taking time off could jeopardize their job or advancement, hence the "workaholic" mentality. Retirement was anticipated, predictable, and achievable for this generation. However, since the economic crash put a serious dent in their retirement accounts (or wiped them out completely) and healthy habits are extending life spans, boomers are living longer and being forced to continue working. As a consequence, this group is not a fan of change. Boomers view training as a path to promotion and value recognition for work well done. Diplomatic, thorough, face-to-face communication is favored; use of modern technology is often avoided. A warm, friendly environment at a company with a valuable mission is usually preferred and fostered by these professionally developed managers and leaders.

And then there are the traditionalists. The legacy of the top-down, hierarchical workplace, and the unquestioning obedience of the industrious traditionalist employee, still perpetuates itself in many workplaces. Quality and dependability are of utmost importance. Also known as the Depression-era kids, their organizations are known for stability and giving back to the community. "Doing more with less" comes out of the need for frugality they experienced. They are loyal and view work as necessary, not necessarily fun. Given the war-era context, a clear chain of command with separation between work and the rest of life—the classic military style—is this generation's organizational model.

With a Gallic shrug, Jean-Baptiste Alphonse Karr intoned, "Plus ça change, plus c'est la même chose" (loosely, "The more things change, the more they stay the same"), and with that pronouncement, Gen Z brings us full circle. According to the NPD study group, Gen Zers prefer home-cooked meals and they aren't big fans of microwave ovens; they would rather use a conventional stove. Gen Z wants to change the world; indeed, 60 percent of its members say they want to have an impact on the world, compared to 39 percent of millennials (according to a study by Sparks & Honey, a New York-based marketing agency). Roughly one in four Gen Zers is already involved in volunteering—college is less important to them. Sixty-four percent of Gen Zers are considering volunteer opportunities compared to 71 percent of millennials. Harkening back to an earlier era, 72 percent of Gen Z high school students want to start a business someday while 61 percent would rather be an entrepreneur than an employee when they graduate college. Further, they are very independent thinkers, not collaborators, according to a joint study by Millennial Branding (a consulting firm) and Internships.com. This recession-era group is the workforce on the horizon; it's the one to watch and plan on engaging for your organization's future. While educational debt is a common experience for many Millennials and Gen Xers, and is projected to be a factor for Gen Z as well, Gen Z seems less amenable to, and sees less value in, accruing such debt and having a career as an employee.

APPLYING YOUR UNDERSTANDING OF GENERATIONAL ATTITUDES

The older generation thought nothing of getting up at five every morning -
and the younger generation doesn't think much of it either.

—JOHN J. WELSH

The stereotypes regarding today's employees are not always accurate be-cause things are not always what they seem. Regardless of which generational group you fall into, it is fundamental for you as a manager and leader to listen to your coworkers and help them communicate with each other better. We all have perceptual "windshields" through which we filter and interpret every-thing, and that blinds us to the true road conditions (the same may be said of our hindsight: "objects in mirror are closer than they appear"). In driving towards our goals, it is easy to get sidetracked by distorted views, and forget that we are not driving alone and others have a useful, different perspective. Your team is there to help you if you empower them to do it in their own way.

Work ethic, lifestyle, loyalty, and respect are actually valued by all of to-day's living generations, though each group sees them differently. Actually, many of the expectations of millennials mirror the desires of employees in every generation, so making changes to satisfy their demands will help bridge the generation gaps. However, a millennial supervisor needs to know how to perpetuate the baby boomers' loyalty and the perseverance of Gen Xers. Boomers can learn a great deal about how to leverage social media and new technologies and Gen Xers can improve their collaboration skills, from their millennial colleagues. Regardless of when you were born, you need to know how to motivate, look after, and lead all types of people on your team.

The reality is each generation feels misunderstood and underappreciated, and has an inherently biased view of themselves. A 2013 Bentley University study of 3,000 millennials and their bosses revealed that 89 percent say they have a strong work ethic, but only 74 percent of non-millennials believe they have as strong a work ethic as that of previous generations. Also, 55 percent of millennials say they're willing to "pay their dues," but 70 percent of non-millennials say that they aren't as willing as they should be.

Every generation brings a new set of habits and strengths to your organization. In addition to a mindset shift, incremental changes to your company's benefits, rewards, job processes, organizational structures, communication methods, and productivity tools are required to tap into the financial benefits of receiving the elusive "discretionary effort" from your employees. For example, millennials are naturally suited for global around-the-clock work—they are flexible, enjoy travel, and thrive in changing environments. They are nimble and offer a wealth of knowledge about technology. Gen Zers will demonstrate many of those attributes plus a greater degree of self-sufficiency.

So what are the top five working style changes required to retain and engage boomers and Gen Xers, as well as meet the demands of millennials?

1. **Establish work policies and processes that facilitate mobile (remote) working.** Many millennials enjoy merging work with personal time and they are willing to put in the time necessary to do a good job, however they are uninterested in "face time." Gen Xers and boomers both have personal demands that frequently require them to work outside the office. Supporting this option only boosts productivity.

2. **Be a real human: get to know your employees as people.** Go out for coffee, a walk, or lunch to just talk with them and inquire about their dreams and aspirations; show them you genuinely care about their ideas, career growth, and success. Millennials love the apprentice approach so allow them to work by your side during a crisis and create other shadow learning opportunities. Gen Xers appreciate this as well—often they become close personal friends with their co-workers and this engenders loyalty that generates benefits beyond increased retention.

3. **Practice two-way mentoring.** Millennials can benefit from guidance on professional communications and decorum, as well independent decision making. Established leaders can learn about how to inspire teams and drive consensus from the natural strengths of millennials. All

generations can draw from each other's traits to determine how best to make the tough calls.

4. **Think and act short-term.** Boomer and Gen X managers have a tendency to lose the interest of their millennial employees by looking too far into the future. Millennials live in present, because their world has proven that nothing is a guarantee—from wholesale layoffs to war—they feel there's not a lot anyone can count on. These world events impacted the attitudes of Gen X employees as well. As a result, today's employees are not interested in promotion plans for five years from now. To reach and retain millennials and other employees, create short-term opportunities with incentives that are certain. This approach speaks to their reality while simultaneously building trust. Reward small successes along the way, string these milestones together, and your staff will stay with you longer. For example, a leading retail organization created the Working Hard Card: when managers witness an employee rising to a challenge, exceeding expectations, or otherwise producing extraordinary outcomes, they can hand the employee a Working Hard Card on the spot. Each card is worth a set amount of paid time off to be used at the employee's discretion. It is a simple strategy that rewards employees in the currency they value most—their time.

5. **Share your organization's purpose and relate it to individual employee's work daily.** Millennials like to know about the roles of others in their organization as well as what the company is up to in the big picture. Take time to update employees on all parts of the company. Create a plan that outlines your team's roles and how they relate to the company's objectives. This will help employees better understand how their work matters and inspire them to engage their creativity and energy to find the best ways to achieve those goals.

Additionally, here are some key phrases to use with the various generations represented in your team:

Phrases that motivate baby boomers:

✓ "We need you." "You can make a difference."

Rewards that motivate baby boomers:

✓ Personal appreciation, promotion, recognition, status symbols

Phrases that motivate Gen Xers:

✓ "Do it your way." "There is life beyond work."

Rewards that motivate Gen Xers:

✓ Free time, upgraded resources, opportunities for development, bottom-line results, certifications to add to resumes

Phrases that motivate millennials:

✓ "We respect you here." "What are your goals?"

Rewards that motivate millennials:

✓ Awards, certificates, tangible evidence of credibility

Management actions that motivate millennials:

✓ Connect job requirements and company goals/mission to their personal and career goals

Top 10 Multi-Generational Best Practices:

1. Identify your organization's generational composition and use that information for engagement efforts

2. Provide channels for open communication and interactive team activities

3. Provide corporate communications and training in a variety of formats

4. Include representatives of all generations on strategic and organizational committees

5. Support continuing education

6. Reward managers for retention

7. Reward performance and productivity in a variety of ways, to provide meaningful options based on individual employees' preferences

8. Offer horizontal movement

9. Offer flexible work schedules and arrangements

10. Provide (at least) weekly performance feedback

Much-needed relationship building could bring the generations closer together. In a recent study by PricewaterhouseCoopers, nearly 40 percent of millennials claimed that older managers don't relate well to younger workers, and 34 percent of them thought their personal drive intimidated members of other generations. Flexibility and respect for the individual, as well as the organization, are good for everyone. Loyalty from younger employees, once earned, is long lasting. In fact, loyalty to modern employees' managers and mentors is the number one reason Gen Xers and millennial employees stay in a job, especially during the first three tenuous years. Dissatisfaction with their direct manager is the number one reason they leave. The investment you make in accommodating the changing attitudes of today's employees will be returned to you more than tenfold with decreased turnover, improved morale and productivity, and measurable financial results. It all starts with improved relationships, and Chapter 5 provides proven techniques and detailed examples of what is working for companies these days.

Chapter 5

RELATIONSHIPS ARE THE UNIVERSAL FUEL

Getting Performance That Generates Results

So much of what we call management consists in
making it difficult for people to work.

—PETER F. DRUCKER,
"the father of modern management"

HOW MANY TIMES HAVE you heard people in your organization (including yourself) complain about broken processes that make it difficult to get anything done? Are there managers or individuals on your team that you or others label as "difficult?" Do certain groups or people in your company have a reputation for being unresponsive roadblocks to avoid? The good news is these are opportunities to improve employee engagement. We all know managers are supposed to remove obstacles, provide focus, and ensure team objectives are met. However, shortcomings often occur for a variety of reasons related primarily to a manager's personal aptitudes and competing demands on time. Every company faces challenges that simply make it harder to for people to get work done. Successful companies—and people—constantly challenge themselves to identify and correct these situations. Let's consider some strategies that will help build and strengthen relationships with and among your colleagues by fostering loyalty, trust, and commitment.

Your role as a leader and manager is to help your employees do their best work, not to simply delegate, give orders or point them in a particular direction. By encouraging your employees to speak up when they see areas for improvement, you build relationships by supporting collaboration and create he possibility of making your work easier. Leveraging their ideas and desire to solve problems drives meaningful performance improvement and a culture of positive, constructive thinking. Your employees know what needs to be done to solve problems they deal with on a regular basis. Moreover, your team will happily spend extra time and effort improving inefficient processes and creating better approaches if they believe you are listening and those changes will be implemented. The fact is they already spend a great deal of time fantasizing and talking about how they would do things differently and how much better it would be if XYZ action could be taken. By trusting your team members with the time, authority, and appropriate budget to make it happen, you will empower them to act as internal entrepreneurs and facilitate driving changes that will benefit your organization in multiple ways.

Internal difficulties typically reflect frustrations your customers experience when dealing with your company. Therefore it behooves you to devote adequate internal-facing resources to equipping your frontline engagement officers (i.e., people managers at all levels) with the tools they need to motivate their team members to deliver high-performance results. Just as it is important for sales and marketing teams to measure and respond to your customers' feedback to ensure their satisfaction (via meeting needs and fulfilling expectations) and loyalty (via positive feeling of getting more than expected), attention must be devoted by managers to ensure employee satisfaction and loyalty.

While studies show that *satisfaction* does not equate to *engagement*, satisfaction is a necessary ingredient in attaining engagement. Based on a

2014 study of 2.2 million employees from 2,100 companies performed by HR Solutions Inc., employee dissatisfaction is often the result of issues with managers and interactions with other departments. In fact, six of the top ten dissatisfaction factors were attributed to organizational barriers to employee success. Specifically, those obstacles include: heavy workloads/understaffing; lack of direction/guidance; poor communication between departments and by management; micromanagement; favoritism/arbitrary/discriminatory treatment; and inadequate resources/tools. However, working cooperatively, you and your teams could resolve eight of the ten most significant factors through improved internal company communications, policies, and processes.

Employees are consistently dissatisfied by managers' and executives' lack of communication—they want you to acknowledge their contributions and update them on the big picture and how their efforts help your objectives. When managers are overworked and understaffed, they are not in a position to fulfill their most important function: engaging and supporting employees in achieving goals that align their professional skills with your company's targets. Managers who are expected to make their own individual contributions realistically do not have the bandwidth to coach and develop their teams; they simply can't accomplish both tasks well. And they certainly do not have time to devote to getting to know people individually, giving frequent feedback, and actively instigating meaningful emotional involvement in your company's mission.

Moreover, when management is the only path for promotion, you wind up with managers who do not want to do what your organization needs supervisors to do. As a consequence of downplaying the traditional role of people management (primary function of motivating people and keeping them informed and involved), your managers and individual contributors become frustrated and disengaged. For those who try to do it all, the overload is a guarantee of burnout, absenteeism, turnover, deflated morale, and quality degradation—all of which increase costs and hurt your bottom line.

You'll likely find that some of your executives, too, are disengaged. According to Gallup, only 36 percent of executives and managers are engaged, and only 41 percent of employees know their company's mission or understand what the company is trying to achieve. Obviously this has a negative impact on your customers' experience and your organization's financial performance. The Gallup *2013 State of the American Workplace* report found that managers who positively and skillfully focus on their employees have a massively beneficial impact by doubling engagement levels and virtually eliminating active disengagement (disgruntled employees). The report also noted that organizations with higher than average numbers of engagement employees also logged 147 percent higher earnings per share. While these numbers are anecdotal, they demonstrate how relationships impact your bottom line and how managers at all levels play a key role in expanding or hindering engagement. As an executive, you need to model values and habits that support relationship building and communication of your company's mission. You need to share your enthusiasm with your employees. Finally, you can take steps to foster trust and collaboration while promoting a sense of community and recognition of achievement throughout your organization. As a manager, you should get to know the strengths and professional goals of your staff, play to their skills and interests, and coach people to achieve higher performance while offering them opportunities and resources to develop to their full potential.

According to Blessing White's 2013 engagement research report, skilled, active management and supportive organizational practices are the key ingredients in fueling successful engagement-inducing cultures. It is common for employees at all levels to complain about managers who do not have the time or the inclination to communicate regularly and fail to provide clear guidance or reply to requests. If you, as a manager, are not responsive to your people, you are probably getting in the way of their progress and hindering their productivity. You may feel unable to give enough attention to your staff, and frustrated by the opposing demands on you to produce while directing others' efforts.

This is (at least partially) an organizational issue. When developing your charges for the mutual benefit of reaching your objectives and furthering theirs becomes just another task on a long list of action items, something needs to change. That is a telltale sign of overload and stress, or of genuine disinterest in managing people. Either way, the avoidance of communication, mentoring, and counseling is a formula for disengagement. Your employees will lose interest and create more problems than they solve if you do not show genuine concern for them—their ideas, struggles, and accomplishments. For example, creating development plans and career growth opportunities for your employees is a win-win that simultaneously boosts retention and productivity while preserving valuable history and "tribal knowledge." Listen to employees who express or demonstrate a lack of desire to manage people; develop their "soft" skills and find other ways to promote or reward those high-performing individual contributors. Take the opinions and concerns of employees about managers seriously and use that information as the basis of coaching opportunities to nurture managers' skills.

Executives, managers, and Human Resources staff, together, need to collaborate on enhancing managers' performance, fueling employees with daily messages about the company's purpose in ways that register with individual employees' values and inspire their commitment to the shared goals. Cultivate professionally personal relationships with your staff and people on teams with whom you work on a daily or weekly basis; learn what excites, worries, and matters to these people and get to know something of their personal life. Human Resources cannot discover and collect this information from all employees through surveys or other initiatives—it is your role as a manager to establish relationships with everyone on your team. It is a managerial responsibility to share information with HR so they can incorporate it into strategic company-wide programs that will be meaningful to employees and mutually beneficial.

Human Resources needs input to support your frontline engagement efforts as a manager. That support takes many forms: recruiting; on-boarding; training and development programs; reward and recognition programs; tools and resource libraries; one-on-one support for sensitive issues; performance metrics and reporting; and so on. If your company's culture reflects values and principles that promote community, its organizational structures and HR programs should be crafted to support relationship building, professional development, and succession planning for retention.

Relationships with your employees are like any other relationship—they require care and feeding. Managers must devote a significant amount of time and thought about how to best support their people so they can contribute at their highest level. Managers must prioritize their time accordingly, and your organization must provide them with ample training, assistance, and bandwidth to realistically enable them to fulfill that function.

It is all too common for well-meaning companies to roll out tools to help managers motivate and reward their people, only to discover they do not get used or are underutilized. Tools are helpful only when people understand how to use them and can actually leverage them. Resource and authority constraints can also crimp your ability to collect thoughtful suggestions for improvement from your staff, or preclude you from synthesizing information you've received and implementing it. Employees will lose faith in your sincerity if you solicit their input but fail to act on that input. The unfortunate reality is that if managers do not have time to sit down and talk with employees on a regular basis, they will also not be able to institute suggested improvements. Similarly, they likely do not have time to take advantage of nifty performance management and other engagement tools.

When your colleagues share their thoughts about how things can be improved, they are engaged and hopeful. Establishing committees and involving your employees at all levels in corporate initiatives (for which they volunteer based on their interest) aimed at inspiring and collecting those thoughts is a great tool for fostering engagement. However, if your employees or managers are not empowered to take action and they do not see any changes, they become jaded. In a best-case scenario, they only become disconnected and reluctant to expend extra energy (discretionary effort) because it is valuable and they do not want to "waste" their time and effort. But in a worst-case reading, your employees become embittered and infect coworkers with those counterproductive feelings. Such actively disengaged employees fuel discontent among those who already believe the engaged employees are "drinking the Kool-Aid." This is why it is critical to directly respond to your employees' suggestions, even when they are unsolicited. Failure to do this sends the message: "Your opinions are not valued; we do not care." This kills involvement, motivation, and creativity.

Do not underestimate the power of likeability. If your employees *like* you, they will do more for you. There is mutual value in maintaining relationships for future opportunities that come out of developing the relationships with your employees. The personal touch is most effective to show appreciation and demonstrate your investment in your employees' well-being. Accordingly, your people managers directly influence the degree to which your employees contribute their energy and ideas towards helping your company achieve its mission and goals. It is essential to train new managers and provide them with guidance about effective management techniques. Micromanagement is a common pitfall of high-performing individual contributors when they are moved up and given teams to manage. Just as *you* do not like to be micromanaged, nobody else does, especially not high performers. The people you want most—because of their stellar capabilities to contribute—chafe under "adult supervision" and it becomes a de-motivating distraction. They want managers who will make their job easier by facilitating higher-level discussions, sharing relevant information, and collaborating as colleagues to come up with solutions to achieve milestones.

Having a flexible, collaborative management style is imperative for leading today's pool of employees. When you are respectful of your team's opinions, your team members will view you as a role model and willingly cooperate with and support you. Being a flexible manager requires you to adopt a mind-set of learning from your employees and viewing your role more as that of facilitator than all-knowing sage or dictator. Additionally, your millennial employees in particular want managers who act like mentors to help them grow and develop professionally.

As a manager today, you need to learn how to manage remote employees. Widely dispersed—indeed, *global*—teams are becoming the norm, and work-from-home arrangements are not only increasingly popular, they are also proven to improve engagement. Gallup's study reported that more remote workers were actively engaged than onsite workers; of those who work remotely about 20 percent of the time, 35 percent are actively engaged and this group has the lowest numbers of actively disengaged workers. The benefits of having skilled managers in your company, who are able to optimize their teams' productivity, will more than compensate for the loss of managers' individual production.

Additionally, your organizational policies, processes, and practices need to support an efficient and fulfilling work environment. Here are some common areas that undercut this objective and create disengagement obstacles:

☐ Clunky or underdeveloped on-boarding processes that fail to provide employees with all of the equipment, information, and basic resources they need to hit the ground running, or fail to establish a dialogue to set expectations, priorities, and goals

☐ Impersonal, form-based performance management processes that are perceived to be meaningless or political in nature

☐ Promotion and career development processes driven solely by immediate company needs, rather than planned succession, growth, employee input, and performance

☐ Bureaucratic reporting processes that are redundant or unnecessary, provide little value, or generate reports that could be simplified and streamlined

☐ Hiring, managing, and firing processes or practices that preclude retention of high performers and lead to interpersonal conflicts, disgruntled employees, absenteeism, loss of productivity, and increased associated costs

These organizational hurdles hinder engagement, but conflicts in the workplace are the mostly costly source of disengagement and performance problems. Chapter 6 takes a closer look at common conflicts between employees and their managers, and amongst co-workers at large, revealing the often ignored conduct giving rise to employment related legal claims and insidiously eating away at profits by promoting absenteeism and turnover. It also provides guidance on how to prevent these tough situations, and solutions for resolving them when they do arise.

Chapter 6

KEEP THE ENGINE RUNNING CLEAN

Eliminate Pollutants That Infect Office Morale

WORKPLACE BULLYING IS AN insidious and costly problem. This occurs when a person (or group of people) in an organization target another person for continuous unreasonable, embarrassing, or intimidating treatment that interferes with the target's ability to perform on the job. The perpetrator may be a co-worker who is insecure, bigoted, or immature. Many times the offender is a person in a position of authority who either dislikes the targeted person or feels threatened by that employee. According to recent statistics, managers at all levels comprise 72 percent of the people who display bullying or uncivil behaviors in the workplace.

Workplace bullying can occur in even the best companies with the most popular cultures. However, many companies unintentionally have a culture that allows or even encourages this kind of behavior. Either way, the reality is this: your company is at risk of incurring increased costs, lower revenues and poor productivity due to workplace bullying, unless deliberate actions are taken to prevent it and resolve conflicts between employees.

The business costs associated with workplace bullying (i.e., employees being subjected to aggression, bigotry, and varying levels of harassment or interference with performance) to mid-size companies (several hundred employees) is substantial; over a two-year period these companies lost more than $180 million in squandered time and productivity alone. Other studies reveal figures of similar consequence to companies with thousands of employees, based on turnover and replacement costs and not including costs of associated legal claims and litigation.

This dramatically demonstrates that kind, respectful, and inclusive communication in the office is not just a "nice to have," it is essential to the success and sustainability of your business. Failure to ensure that your employees are safe from emotional, verbal, and physical abuse not only opens you up to liability—it kills morale, reduces productivity, increases costs, and decreases profitability. It also damages your company's reputation. Many companies are unaware of the magnitude of this problem, while others know it exists, but continue to struggle with prevention and management of these incidents when they arise.

The pervasive nature of workplace bullying makes it difficult to distinguish from typical conflicts that arise from misunderstandings and differences of opinion. Sometimes bullying is subtle and difficult to prove, while other times it is blatant, but accepted as "just the way that person is"—an alpha-dog that must be handled with care. To guard against counterproductive, unhealthy conflicts and take appropriate and timely action, you and your fellow managers must be aware of the signs. Workplace bullying can take many forms, including actions that are not often considered in adult contexts:

☐ Shouting; swearing; belittling; stereotyping; subjecting to inappropriate jokes or barbs; or otherwise verbally abusing an employee

☐ Singling out an employee for public ridicule, or unjustified criticism or blame

- [ ] Excluding an employee from company or team activities or similar discriminatory behavior

- [ ] Purposely being dismissive or giving another person credit for an employee's work or contributions

- [ ] Instigating practical jokes, especially if they target the same person.

- [ ] Personal attacks, such as yelling, threats and rumors, as well as manipulation tactics, such as isolation, sabotage (including very subtle tactics like rolling their eyes when a person speaks or "forgetting" to invite the target to important meetings) and micromanagement.

- [ ] Negative comments or actions based on a person's gender, ethnicity, religion, sexual orientation, or other legally protected status. This constitutes harassment and unlike bullying is patently illegal in the United States, giving the targeted employee grounds for a lawsuit.

- [ ] Overloading a targeted employee with an unmanageable volume of work to set them up for failure

- [ ] Giving a worker menial, uninteresting tasks to perform (or no work at all)

- [ ] Purposely setting unrealistic, unclear, or changing goals and deadlines

- [ ] Intentionally distorting the words and actions of others or spreading rumors

- [ ] Arbitrarily or continually denying appropriate requests for leave/vacation

- [ ] Intentionally provoking a targeted employee to quit by creating a hostile or otherwise untenable work environment

You may be thinking, "Bullying is only a problem for children; adults need to learn to deal with crude behavior and develop a thicker skin—it's just a fact of life; suck it up and stop whining." While it's true that everyone needs to learn how to get along with all kinds of people in the workplace, it is simply unnecessary, financially detrimental, and professionally irresponsible to permit bullying in the workplace. In fact, it is illegal in several countries around the world (including the UK, Canada, and Australia) and many states in the US have introduced legislation to address this abusive behavior. According to the Workplace Bullying Institute (yes, there really is such an organization), up to a third of all workers may fall victim to workplace bullying and approximately 20 percent of such activity rises to the level of illegal harassment. *New York Times* research found that approximately 60 percent of workplace bullies are men, and they tend to bully male and female employees equally (female bullies are more likely to bully other females).

Bullying in the workplace has a major financial impact on business in a variety of ways, most notably higher insurance costs related to increased illness (due to stress and its physical effects), disability, absenteeism, and legal claims.

To provide further insight into workplace bullying, a New Jersey-based human resources firm surveyed a broad range of US employees in 2012. Participants ranged in age from their early 20s to late 60s and worked at companies with rosters ranging from fewer than 50 employees to over 5,000 employees in the following industries: technology; education; energy; health care; manufacturing; nonprofits; retail; and professional services. More than 80 percent of those surveyed said that based on their direct experience as a victim or witness, bullying is a serious problem in the workplace. In contrast, the survey revealed that fewer than 25 percent of US-based companies take any action to curb workplace bullying. Ironically, employees who bully others often see themselves as the victim; their behavior can be bold and abrasive or passive-aggressive.

Here are some of the negative financial impacts of workplace bullying:

☐ **High turnover**—which increases costs associated with hiring and training new employees, only to lose them to competitors

☐ **Low productivity**—since employees are distracted and out sick more frequently with stress-related illnesses

☐ **Lost synergies**—because teamwork is diminished, so there is less collaboration, cooperation, and brainstorming, which in turn curtails problem-solving and innovation

☐ **Difficulty in hiring quality employees**—as word spreads that the company has a hostile work environment

☐ **Increased insurance costs**—due to the myriad of health issues associated with bullying

☐ **Costs of litigation**—and related expenses incurred in managing complaints by disgruntled employees

Additionally, bullying behavior causes a ripple effect emanating out from the victim to include witnesses and other innocent bystanders. The result is active disengagement within your organization and damage to your company's reputation. Affected employees can suffer in many ways:

1. Stress-induced uncharacteristically antisocial behavior

2. Absenteeism and low productivity

3. Lowered self-esteem and depression

4. Anxiety

5. Digestive upsets

6. High blood pressure

7. Insomnia

8. Trouble with relationships resulting from work-related stress

9. Post traumatic stress disorder

In 2010, the Workplace Bullying Institute conducted a survey in the US that yielded some sober statistics:

✓ 35 percent of the US workforce (~ 53.5 million Americans) report being bullied at work

✓ An additional 15 percent witness bullying

✓ Both men and women engage in bullying

✓ 62 percent of bullies are men

✓ 58 percent of targets are women

✓ 68 percent of bullying is targeted at the same gender

✓ Women bully other women in 80 percent of cases

✓ Bullying is four times more prevalent than illegal harassment

Research conducted by the European Foundation for the Improvement of Living and Working Conditions (Eurofound) had similar findings, while adding a few additional points:

✓ Bullied employees had higher levels of work-induced illness (such as stress, anxiety, and irritability)

✓ Office bullying correlated with higher than average rates of absenteeism

✓ Company culture or job factors contributing to bullying behavior include low levels of control over one's work, high levels of work intensity (tight deadlines, fast-paced environment), and frequent contact with unaffiliated individuals (customers, clients, etc.)

The defining characteristic of workplace bullying (as opposed to garden-variety office politics) is the impact on employees' health and associated costs to your organization. The Workplace Bullying Institute's study highlighted the seven most common health issues:

✓ Anxiety, stress, excessive worry (76 percent)

✓ Loss of concentration (71 percent)

✓ Disrupted sleep (71 percent)

✓ Feeling edgy, irritable, easily startled, and constantly on guard (60 percent)

✓ Stress headaches (55 percent)

✓ Obsessing over minute details at work (52 percent)

✓ Recurrent memories, nightmares and flashbacks (49 percent)

This issue of workplace bullying speaks directly to the "human" element of human resources. Since a single employee and your organization's culture has such a profound emotional and physical impact on other employees (which is reflected in their performance and retention), it is essential to establish and enforce positive policies and practices regarding communication and interactions. You need to be sensitive to the perceptions and triggers of your diverse group of employees to do that effectively. While your intentions, or those of the person delivering the message, may be good or pure, it is the interpretation by the person on the receiving end that counts towards the bottom-line business results. Employees report feeling bullied when they are regularly subjected to comments that reflect biases and stereotyping. One of the easiest ways to alienate and upset your coworkers is to make assumptions, use stereotypes, and say inappropriate things. These micro-aggressions have a compounding effect. Below are some lists of common actions and statements that offend various gender and ethnic groups (compiled by Diversity Inc.):

✓ Do not assume ethnicity or skills and preferences based on skin color or appearance.

✓ "You don't act very [fill in the group]."

✓ "What's your name again?" [Listen carefully the first time—it's OK to ask for spelling or check your pronunciation]

✓ "You all look alike."

✓ "You are all bad drivers"

✓ "Can you speak your language?"

✓ "You speak so well [for your _____]"

Women find these comments unwelcome and disrespectful:

1. **Terms of "endearment" such as "sweetie," "hon" or "cutie."** This is viewed as degrading and belittling.

2. **"You've lost weight," or "You look so much better." "You look too young to have all that experience."** Compliments like this offered to a female candidate, employee, or executive—especially publicly or at an inappropriate moment—can make her feel as though her skills and work are not taken seriously or viewed as credible, because of the focus on her appearance. Men typically do not face this at work, and neither should women.

3. **Any kind of sexual comment.** Not only do sexual innuendos and intimate terms like "honey" make female employees feel embarrassed and offended, they also create an atmosphere of inequality and disrespect that becomes a problem for other employees and can cross the line into illegal sexual harassment.

4. **"Is it that time of the month?" or "She's so emotional," or "You wear your heart on your sleeve."** This perpetuates the preconceived notion that women cannot handle stress and tend to get too emotional, whereas men are viewed as "passionate" and "assertive" leaders. When a female executive has a commanding presence, it is often viewed in a negative way, whereas when a man in the same position acts that way he is just perceived as doing his job.

5. **"You aren't as aggressive or assertive as you should be. You need to be more forceful and tougher." "You don't sound confident."** "These are code words for being more 'manly,'" says Barbara Frankel, senior vice president and executive editor of DiversityInc. There are many different successful management and communication styles. In fact studies have shown that communication strengths commonly associated with women (e.g., collaboration, listening) are more effective in business today.

6. **"You only got the job because you're a woman."** This will never send a positive message. If you want to show you are encouraging gender diversity, you might simply say something like, "we target qualified people with diverse backgrounds."

7. **"Do you really want that promotion? You'll never see your kids." "Do you want to keep working now that you're married [divorced, pregnant, your husband/partner is relocating, your husband/partner is retiring]?"** These questions reflect underlying biases or stereotypes about women and their attitudes towards work. They also set women up for career advancement hurdles and contribute to a male-dominated corporate culture, which encourages women to move on rather than contribute their talents and energy to a dead-end proposition.

8. **"You do that so well for a girl."** Even jokingly, the phrase implies that women are inferior to men and reinforces dated stereotypes. It

also discourages many young women from staying in male-dominated teams and organizations, especially in roles requiring STEM degrees. Any conversation that implies that a woman—or any individual from any group—is somehow an anomaly or "less than" is inappropriate and discriminatory.

9. **"Are you pregnant?" or "When are you due?"** Until a coworker decides to bring it up on her own, it is not an appropriate conversation for work.

Asians (and members of any other ethnic group) do not appreciate stereotype-based comments:

1. **"You speak English well. Where did you learn it?"** While this may be meant as a compliment, it implies that you anticipate communication problems with someone based on their ethnic heritage.

2. **"You need to improve your communication skills."** This is usually code for "I can't understand you because you have an accent." With globalization, there are increasing numbers of experienced, high-performing professionals who speak English with accents. We all need to learn to listen and make an effort to understand each other. Dinging someone in a performance review for "poor" or "needs improvement" communications skills on the basis of an accent is not helpful to the employee or your organization. This fosters a homogenous culture, which limits performance and opportunities for innovation and business growth.

3. **"Asians are not discriminated against. All of my doctors are Asian, and the Asian kids in school are the ones getting top honors. It's the white kids who are at a disadvantage."** Even positive stereotypes are damaging: The myth that all Asians are good at and want a career in medicine, math, and science is limiting. Additionally, you should never assume what role an Asian—or any person—plays in an organization.

4. **"Asians are good workers but seldom want to become leaders."** There's a strong stereotype that while Asians are good individual performers, they lack certain leadership qualities because they are "passive" or "quiet." The beliefs reflect a lack of cultural competence. Many Asian Americans with strong non-Western cultural roots might have a quiet leadership style, more behind-the-scenes than what is considered mainstream.

The solution? Draw attention to a variety of successful leaders and management styles.

5. **"Can you recommend a good [Chinese, Thai, Vietnamese, Indian, sushi, etc.] restaurant?"** Don't ask for dining recommendations based on ethnicity or assume, for example, that someone of Indian descent is vegetarian or prefers Indian food—that is often not the case, and the person may be offended by what was intended as a benign query.

6. **Do not assume your employee's country of origin; you might be wrong.** Guessing appears arrogant and dismissive, rather than informed and respectful. Err on the side of curiosity and simply ask, but only under appropriate circumstances. Upon first meeting or during an interview is not appropriate.

7. **"Where are you from originally?" "How often do you go home/visit your family?"** The first question implies that any person with an accent is an outsider, and both questions are invasive and based on stereotyped assumptions.

5 Ways You Can Prevent Stereotypes

1. Don't perpetuate stereotypes—even positive ones.

2. Offer opportunities for professional development to all your employees equally.

3. Offer your employees stretch assignments and opportunities based on their input and actual performance, not on assumptions based on preconceived notions.

4. Assign cross-cultural mentors and expand the purpose of ethnic or gender-based resource groups beyond sharing cultural practices and holidays. Create a more inclusive mission and opportunities for information exchanges with other groups and employees-at-large.

5. Draw attention to successful role models that defy and disprove stereotypes.

Statements to avoid saying to a veteran, or assuming about veterans:

1. "Thank you for your service, but I don't think we should have been there in the first place."

2. "Why did you join? The military is a job for men."

3. "You're too rigid to deal with sudden changes."

4. "You're a mother/wife, how could you leave your family while you were deployed?"

5. "How did your husband/boyfriend/significant other feel about you being around all those men?"

6. "Do you have PTSD?"

7. "What's the worst thing that happened to you over there?"

This is like asking someone, "What's the worst day of your life? Tell me in detail"–no one wants to do that.

8. "Have you ever killed anyone?"

9. "Were you raped?"

According to the Workplace Bullying Institute's research, only 13 percent of bullies are reprimanded despite management's awareness of the magnitude of the problem. If this sort of disconnect exits in your organization, it is clear that employees and managers who bully others are not being held accountable for disrupting the team. This perpetuates the problem, expands negative impacts, and increases the measurable and unmeasurable costs to your company. What is the best way to deal with office bullying?

A report by Canada's Safety Council states that organizations that manage people properly outperform those who do not by 30 to 40 percent. Being aware of the signs and symptoms of bullying helps you and your organization take proactive steps to prevent it, or intervene before matters escalate. Communication, elimination of bias, and leadership training should be provided to employees at all levels to raise awareness and educate people about inappropriate office behavior (beyond the legally required sexual harassment training). Additionally, create policies defining and prohibiting bullying conduct, outlining a process to report bullying, and prescribing appropriate disciplinary actions. These policies will only be effective if they are enforced. Managers and HR must take complaints seriously, investigate them thoroughly, and act on them in a timely manner—ideally by providing coaching to both the individual accused of bullying and the victim. It is common for bullies to report being victims of discriminatory or other inappropriate behavior, further complicating the issue. The best way to respond to these matters is to hire outside coaches who have experience dealing with workplace bullying. Avoid making statements like, "There really isn't anything we can do," or "You'll just have to deal with it." The fact is there are many actions that can and should be taken to resolve it, for the benefit of your people and your company's performance. All executives must be diligent in setting the right tone, modeling appropriate behaviors and creating a culture that embraces a "zero tolerance" for workplace bullying.

Finally, it is important to realize that the US is the last of the western democracies to adopt laws forbidding bullying conduct in the workplace. Scandinavian nations have had explicit anti-bullying laws since 1994. Many of the European Union nations have substantially more legal employee protections compelling employers to prevent or correct bullying. The UK, the country that coined the term "workplace bullying," has broader anti-harassment laws than the US that also cover bullying. Ireland has a strong health and safety code that addresses bullying. Canada has anti-bullying laws, and in 2011, Australia passed the first *criminal* statute prohibiting workplace bullying. It is only a matter of time before your company will be legally required to prohibit and respond to bullying. Proactively addressing this will place your company in a leadership role with a reputation of having an enlightened, high-performance corporate culture that truly embraces diversity, and all of the financial benefits that come from a productively engaged workforce. Next, in Chapter 7, discover how best to introduce and implement lasting changes that future proof your organization.

Chapter 7

SUCCESSFUL CHANGE MANAGEMENT

Maintaining A Smooth Transmission While Shifting Gears

Change is hard because people overestimate the value of what they have—and underestimate the value of what they may gain by giving that up.

—JAMES BELASCO and Ralph Stayer, *Flight of the Buffalo*

CHANGE MANAGEMENT IS AN exercise in engaging people; it's a process, not an event. We all know that meaningful changes do not happen overnight, especially in corporate organizations, and according to several studies, 70 percent of all organizational change attempts fail. There are many reasons for this, but the root cause is *fear*. Since people drive organizations, it is imperative for you as a manager and leader to deal with this natural, biological emotion that impacts and ultimately determines the success or failure of organizational changes you want to make.

Change is fundamentally uncomfortable, difficult, and scary. However, change cannot and should not be avoided; indeed, it is necessary to stay relevant and competitive in business. And change can in fact be a positive thing: people actually crave new and different experiences and are motivated by opportunities to make a difference. The key to successful change management is *facilitation*. In addition to outlining a change facilitation process, in this chapter we will point out the fatal errors that impede transitions, as well as revealing the underpinnings of transformations that stick and pay off.

In order to get the necessary buy-in from your employees, you need to leverage their desires and commitment to the organization's success. In addition to the instinctual human reactions to change, a flawed approach is the other primary reason change management efforts frequently fail. According to PWC's 2013 change management survey results, 84 percent of the 2,200 companies in the study viewed culture as being critically important to success, but less than 50 percent of those companies leverage or consider culture when making changes. Equally telling, 70 percent of the companies who reported successful change efforts said they incorporated cultural values with which their employees identified. Less than half of the study's participants saw their respective company's culture as being consistent with the proposed shifts and transitions their organizations tried to institute. Clearly, your company's culture is critical to its successful growth and evolution. Consider how your contemplated course of action aligns with your company's culture—will it improve the culture? If you believe your culture is what attracts and keeps great employees, will this change be in potential conflict with how your team manifests that culture?

There are numerous valid reasons for reevaluating internal structures and processes and making changes in your team or strategy. Employees understand and appreciate this and, when such adjustments are handled properly, workers actually welcome them. Of course, as a practical matter, you need your employees to carry out the new ways of doing things and continue to execute under different conditions. The best way to ensure your team is on board with departures from a known, established system under which they are accustomed to operating, is to involve them in the decision-making process. People are more receptive to trying new things when they feel it is a choice rather than a directive. There are many ways you can include employees throughout your company in even the most high-level decisions. For example, if you are considering a reorganization that will affect several departments in your company and possibly result in elimination of some roles and creation of new ones, you may be tempted to discuss this with as few people as possible. This is likely to make people feel surprised, confused, and angry because they are handed a fait accompli, or they feel mistrustful and scared because of rumors and the fact that information was withheld. These feelings will cause entrenched resistance rather than general acceptance and create unnecessary distractions. On the other hand, if you at least inform your employees of specific challenges your company faces, and advise them of the need to take actions in response to those challenges, you are helping them understand why they need to work differently.

Open, honest, and proactive communication will mentally prepare your people to adopt course corrections. This also applies to the prevention of disruptions to productivity caused by post-acquisition integrations, organizational growth, as well as strategic, process, policy, and management changes. Including your employees in the real-time conversation about how things are evolving, how that affects their roles, and what ideas are being explored to improve your organization's ability to serve customers, demonstrates that you respect them. By keeping them informed during the decision-making process, you are acknowledging that they matter and you are aware that they will be impacted. Moreover, transitions are a perfect opportunity to solicit ideas and information from your employees—they are your feet on the street with direct experience and valuable insights about what needs improvement and what is feasible. Invite employees to participate in the changes, but only after you explain the objectives you are trying to achieve.

Your company's culture can help make the invitation an inspiring opportunity to participate in problem-solving and creating value. Before crafting that message, assess your organization's operational strengths and weaknesses, and be sure to avoid the mafia boss invitation of making your employees "an offer they can't refuse." When your employees' suggestions are incorporated into the changes and how they are implemented, you greatly increase acceptance and adoption. This also strengthens your organization by increasing engagement, since change is an opportunity to reignite your team's interest and commitment. It is human nature to have an ambivalent relationship with change: it is both scary and exciting. If you alleviate fears and instill enthusiasm, you can employ your people to propel your company forward.

As an executive or manager, you will also experience some reticence or resistance to change. That is natural, so anticipate resistance and prepare for it. Just as change is a double-edged sword, so is resistance. An ancient proverb advises that we can only lean against that which resists. Resistance can therefore serve as a useful form of inquiry or examination, but it should not become an excuse for inertia. Resistance is unavoidable and will always be present in the face of change, so best to expect it and welcome it. Like a martial arts master, turn that energy into an asset by proactively leveraging it. Resistance does not mean that the proposed change is bad, and it does not necessarily mean that those resisting change need to "get out of the way" or that they should be dismissed. In fact, assessing resistance to a proposed change in your organization is a valuable method of simultaneously soliciting input and gathering information that will help you present it in a positive and reassuring way. You can start by telling your employees the story of how you got to the present state, so they can relate to them the company's need to take corrective action. Share your clear objectives and priorities and then ask for their feedback and ideas on how best to achieve the goals. Obviously, a coordinated effort will be required to gather your employees' responses and evaluate them, to gauge the degree of resistance and the reasons for it.

When you experience friction or lack of cooperation from your employees, consider that they may not grasp what it is you want them to do. According to a Katzenbach Center study, 44 percent of employees don't understand a change they are asked to make (reported no clear direction given), yet only 38 percent actually disagree with the decision. Moreover, 65 percent of the more than 2,200 executives, managers, and employees surveyed cited "change fatigue" from multiple simultaneous change initiatives, as the problem. Further, fully half of the respondents said their company did not have the resources and capabilities to execute the desired changes. All of these obstacles are related to another commonly reported issue: failure to include lower-level employees in developing and executing change plans. This further supports the need for leaders and HR to adopt an inclusive, collaborative approach to driving organizational changes. You are essentially assured greater cooperation, productivity, and performance by consulting with your employees before rolling out new procedures or organizational structures. Moreover, by seeking input and consensus, you automatically reduce your chances of running into the common potholes that derail attempts to change course or evolve.

Avoiding the following mistakes will help you optimize your change management strategies and facilitate the success of any new initiative:

☐ Pursuing unrealistically short time frames. Reactive, rushed arrangements are set- ups for failure and preclude participation, communication, and thoughtful consideration, and cannot be truly strategic. When changes are rushed, employees become suspicious, cynical, and disengaged.

☐ Fanfare without follow-through. Do not announce anything new until resources are in place and there is an established timeframe to execute, otherwise you lose credibility and momentum.

☐ Failure to communicate effectively. No one likes to be blind-sided; take steps to discuss anticipated changes with all impacted employees and invite their input.

☐ Inability to anticipate resistance and head it off.

☐ Failure to make a compelling case for the change. Employees need your help to make sense out of the changes.

☐ Making assumptions about people's reactions. You must expect different opinions and devote time and effort to understanding other viewpoints, as well as clearly articulating yours.

☐ Ignoring your organization's existing culture and resources. They will
be needed to support the changes. Culture trumps strategy. Never
underestimate the power of the status quo.

☐ Forgetting that change is a process with several intermediate milestones.
Focus on short-term goals and remain flexible so you can adjust plans
along the way to make course corrections as necessary; there's always more
than one route to a destination.

☐ Failure to leverage relationships in effecting change. Structures and
policies do not change behavior—emotions and relationships do. Getting
people to change behavior requires managerial expertise that differs from
strategic decision-making and other leadership skills.

☐ Looking at the wrong indicators of success or measurements of progress.
You can be led astray by problems that do not actually mean the change is
wrong, unproductive or unnecessary.

☐ Failure to address employees' emotions. This is the most frequently
overlooked piece. The human factor must be taken into account: your
employees fears and concerns must be acknowledged and managed.

Successfully executed changes result from a plan that meets the following
four criteria:

1. Alignment of interests

2. Shared understanding of the reasons behind the change

3. Clear vision of the destination (i.e., what specific goal your company
   hopes to achieve)

4. Compelling story showing how the proposed change will help realize
   that vision

In summary, the traditional approach to change management is not working. Culture and consensus-based approaches are proving more effective; they
are likely to be the only successful approach moving forward, given the nature
of modern employees. Most existing change management methods do not give
enough attention to the human factor, particularly the emotions—like fear and

excitement—that drive behavior. By incorporating processes that deal with those emotions as an element of your change management initiatives, you will not only increase your company's ability to make necessary changes, you will improve the outcomes. More information about how you can augment change initiatives, to ensure you always incorporate the 4 success criteria, is available at www.employeeandclientengagement.com. Next, Chapter 8 lays out a workable approach to performance management, that addresses many of the common challenges associated with it.

Chapter 8

NAVIGATING THE PERFORMANCE MANAGEMENT LANE

Optimizing Modern Employees' Productivity

To handle yourself, use your head. To handle others, use your heart.

—ELEANOR ROOSEVELT

THE KEY TO SUCCESSFULLY motivating your employees is to approach every management initiative and every employee interaction with care, as if you or your closest kin were personally on the receiving end. Look at performance management broadly as the amalgamation of everything that touches your employees at work, and consider how each experience can improve their productivity, engagement, and loyalty. In other words, view it as a way to facilitate and measure the employee experience your company provides and the results that generates. Just as marketers concern themselves with the total customer experience and take advantage of every opportunity to create a positive impression in the mind of buyers, performance management is the process of creating a work environment that inspires people to deliver their best. In turn, the company's performance will benefit measurably; employee engagement moves the needle.

Performance management is much more than a way to collect, evaluate, and respond to isolated metrics. It is a continuous way of studying and optimizing the whole work ecosystem; it begins when each required role is identified and scoped, and continues throughout the tenure of each employee in those roles within your organization. It includes the manner in which you handle every departure of an employee who leaves your team (voluntarily or involuntarily). Executives, managers, and HR should be working together to create and implement functional structures and programs that equip your employees to intelligently drive, and map the progress of, your corporate objectives. Ideally it is imbedded into daily operations and processes, rather than an added box to check.

Modern performance management comprises a company-wide system based on principles that mesh with your organization's culture:

- ☐ Clear roles and responsibilities (with specific goals/performance plans) for each employee and function

- ☐ An appropriate employee selection process that attracts diverse people who are well-suited to helping your company carry out its objectives

- ☐ Unambiguous performance requirements with results-based evaluations (of key result areas/KRAs) and measures, consistent with regular feedback and guidance given to employees

- ☐ Organized and timely orientation process and availability of tools and information employees need to do their job

- ☐ Ongoing career and performance coaching and feedback, including 360-degree evaluations of employees at all levels, educational programs, and professional development training, and mentoring opportunities

- ☐ Quarterly semiformal performance development discussions

☐ Compensation and recognition systems that align incentives and employee skills and interests with corporate objectives, including meaningful rewards to people for their contributions

☐ Promotional/career development opportunities to broaden and augment skills and experience with or without pay increase

☐ Exit interviews for all departing employees (regardless of reason/circumstances) to gain a better understanding of why an employee would choose to leave your organization, as well as candid feedback about the employee experience at your company

Your aim as a leader and manager, regardless of your function or title, is to improve your company's work environment in order to elicit optimal employee productivity, morale, and performance. This requires an emphasis on teamwork in the sports context of supporting each individual's efforts to bring home the win. Trust must be ingrained. If you establish a framework in which everyone gets rewarded or no one gets rewarded, it is easier to establish trust and collaboration. Having clear, shared goals that everyone works together to achieve and a system that rewards all contributors when those goals are met is essential.

Additionally, a more coordinated and personalized approach to attaining individual goals encourages cooperative behavior that motivates every individual to contribute to the collective effort. For example, if a team accomplishes its objective, but some individual members took extraordinary steps to ensure success, those "star players" should be publicly acknowledged (say, with an MVP award). Additionally, individual goals should be clearly articulated and shared with the team. The secrecy that shrouds traditional goal setting processes is unnecessary and counterproductive. Teamwork is fostered when employees understand the demands and priorities incumbent upon their colleagues. As a corollary, successful companies with transparent salary models that allow employees (and job candidates) to openly discuss this touchy subject are proving that colleagues can handle, and prefer, such candor (we neither advocate nor discourage this approach). By encouraging individual achievement within the context of group performance, you foster a results orientation that boosts overall company performance.

Concealing information in the name of corporate confidentiality needlessly creates a cloak and dagger atmosphere that is distracting to employees and invites misunderstandings and conflict. Your employees talk to each other—they probe each other for information and engage in speculation about promotions and the like. They form alliances to share rumors and leaked "facts," and they speculate on upcoming events. This is wasted time and energy that can be redirected into constructive endeavors. If you approach performance management as a process for ongoing communication between executives, managers, and their employees, you will help your team focus on fulfilling the company's objectives and enable the team to measure its success.

A Gallup study of 100,000 employees from 2,500 organizations focused on the relationship between performance management practices and employee attitudes in highly productive work groups. Employee beliefs are influenced by performance management and were found to directly influence productivity and overall employee turnover rates, as well as customer satisfaction. Employees in work groups believed to be "desirable" reported high levels of agreement with the following statements that represent the four pillars (planning, developing, monitoring, and rewarding) of the systematic performance management we recommend:

✓ I know what is expected of me at work.

✓ At work, I have the opportunity to do what I do best every day.

✓ In the last six months, someone at work has talked to me about my progress.

✓ There is someone at work who encourages my development.

✓ I have the materials and equipment I need to do my work right.

✓ This year, I have had opportunities at work to learn and grow.

✓ In the last seven days, I have received recognition or praise for doing good work.

Another prominent survey, "Attracting and Retaining High-Technology Talent," co-sponsored by William M. Mercer, Inc. and the Pittsburgh High Technology Council, highlights best practices for retaining experienced and productive employees:

✓ giving challenging work assignments

✓ offering career development opportunities

✓ providing incentives under variable pay arrangements

This all means you must understand and respect your employees, and openly communicate with them, in order to manage their performance. Accordingly, time invested in periodically setting and evaluating clear expectations and goals that are aggressive yet attainable will pay big dividends. When you understand what motivates your employees, you can effectively communicate and interact with them and build mutual expectations for success. To that end, it is critical to be realistic, open, and honest with your employees and invite them to return this courtesy. For example, accept that many of your youngest employees are not interested in climbing the corporate ladder and embrace their true motivations—securing a source of reliable spending money, for example—and use that to your advantage. When you tell an employee, "I understand this is not your 'forever' job or company, but to earn the paycheck every week, here is what I expect of you," they are much more likely to respond favorably than if you try to motivate with irrelevant promises of promotions and titles down the road.

There will of course be many opportunities to motivate them in ways that are more satisfying to you than that extreme, but real, example. Nonetheless, performance management practices should meet your employees where they are. If an employee views a particular role as a stepping-stone, get that out on the table—make it OK—and work with the fact that they have an opportunity to gain valuable experience by doing a great job in their current role. Allow room for creativity and flexibility in your performance management processes to yield the outcomes you desire. And on that point, keep in mind that high-performance facilitation tools and methods reflect the modern reality that being physically present in the office to do a job is not always necessary.

Incorporate remote work options in order to attract and retain valuable employees as well as promote diversity (especially gender diversity). Today's employees, of all generations, are busier than ever attempting to balance personal and professional demands. Work–life integration is the new balance and providing employees the ability to set their own schedule is key, especially in retaining experienced employees who are parents. Many fortune 500 companies offer perks and amenities "on campus" to encourage and assist employees in striking that balance while in the office, however, the feasibility of such benefits is limited for both employers and employees. Enabling your employees to be productive remotely opens up new opportunities for motivation, retention, and reward, as well as cost savings and increased productivity.

The fact is, modern employees can not only be trusted to work from home, they are often more productive when they work that way. According to the GlobalWorkplaceAnalytics 2013 research report, between 2005 and 2013, remote working arrangements grew by 80 percent in the US, and employee engagement is 55 percent higher among employees who have the flexibility to work remotely. Moreover, stress levels of employees who don't have remote work options are twice as high as those who do. Enabling your employees to work outside the office also improves retention and job satisfaction: 79 percent of US employees stated that would like to work from home at least part of the time. Nearly 60 percent of employees who currently work this way say they would leave their job if they could not telecommute at least some of the time.

Remote work arrangements could save your company an average of $11,000 per employee, per year while effectively providing an additional $2,000–$7,000 to an employee's annual compensation. And not having to commute enables your employees to devote more time to work; employees who work remotely often put in more productive hours for their employer. Technology to ensure remote connectivity is widely available now, and employees increasingly expect and demand such arrangements. For all these reasons and more, flexible and remote working models are increasingly becoming an added dimension of variable pay incentives.

Performance management must be regarded broadly and applied as a proactive, fully integrated system that helps motivate individuals and teams to achieve your organization's desired performance levels, objectives and goals. Its purpose is to facilitate striking an equipoise between individual and organizational objectives and measure results in real-time. The payoff of an approach that gratifies your employees' professional aspirations while respecting their personal commitments is this: they will be loyal and self-motivated to help your organization succeed. That's the concept behind tools for modern performance management, but what about a practical framework or processes to get greater results and ensure your company's success over the long haul? Read on...

Chapter 9

HIGH-PERFORMANCE MODEL

Strategic Nuts And Bolts For A Custom Build

Enjoying success requires the ability to adapt. Only by being open to change will you have a true opportunity to get the most from your talent.

—NOLAN RYAN, American athlete, businessman, and CEO

YOUR ORGANIZATION'S DESTINY IS predictable and controllable. It is a certainty that if you as a leader, and your business as a vehicle, are not developing, adapting, and growing, then it is only a matter of time before your company will stall, shrink and fail. The flexibility and innovation required to keep up with changes in the market are only achievable through rock-solid team effort. Your company's management structures, policies, and practices either support or undermine teamwork. How well your employees work together will determine the profitability and viability of your enterprise. There are many examples of large, established, once-successful companies that made history, then became history—quaint lore or case studies in business books. Countless are the examples of start-ups and smaller companies that struggled for years but never took hold in the marketplace, or were flashes-in-the-pan. Most of these failures were not because of inferior products or bad ideas, but rather, due to the way people were managed and resources were applied. That is not news; you know it to be true.

Here's the news: structuring your company around your people—rather than constraining your options by picking people based on a limited view of your company—will future-proof your organization to keep it relevant and valuable in the face of changing times. If your organization is still creating prescriptive job descriptions that include rigid experience and educational achievement requirements, or hiring, evaluating, and firing people in basically the same way companies have done since the 1900s, your company is in trouble. If your company follows the common cycle of laying people off when their jobs are technically eliminated, then creating new positions and hiring different people to fill them, you are throwing away money and other valuable resources. Your organization will not attract and retain top performers and you will perpetually waste time and effort demolishing and rebuilding teams, instead of *developing* them to focus on innovation and delivering quality products and services for your customers. The key to doing this is to ENHANCE employee engagement.

As a preliminary matter, it is essential to address work arrangements, since more employees of all generations are increasingly expecting and requiring a sustaining, more balanced way of life. Robert Morgan of the Hudson Highland Group noted, "Money will always be important to people, but in this age of Internet powered remote access where there are so many virtual options, employees place a much higher premium on flexible work arrangements." In 2008, a third of the workforce cited flexibility and lifestyle as their number one priority and most important factor in considering where to work, based on survey data collected by Rasmussen Reports. Ever since, the percentage of employees who identify flexibility as their first priority is increasing year after year, because the values of younger workers and the needs of older workers are converging into a shared demand for more fluid schedules. Moreover, many millennials do not want to work for someone else forever; the most ambitious members of this demographic ultimately want to have their own business. Early indications are that this entrepreneurial spirit is engrained in the generation following them as well—Gen Z. Where entrepreneurs used to be exceptional and most working-age people could be counted on to simply desire employment, that old status quo is being stood on its head. To attract, keep and motivate talent, your organization will need to engage people with a new mindset.

Gone are the days of unquestioning loyalty to a company, but this does not mean you should assume or accept that today's employees will be less committed to your company. Today's employees are inclined to be more invested in the success of the company they work for, especially if the company's mission is aligned with their values in some way. Long-term employees are more valuable than ever because now they are a competitive edge, and studies indicate that employees often provide more valuable contributions over more time with the same company. Additionally, studies show that experienced workers, regardless of gender, are most productive in their 40's and 50's, so it behooves you to attract and retain a diverse demographic of employees. To get and keep engaged employees, as a manager and leader, you must change certain expectations you have about where and how employees work, as well as perceptions about what productivity looks like.

Technology and modern habits enable people to be equally as productive on the go as they are at their desk in the office. In fact, mobile computing and smartphones have forever changed the way people work. The home is no longer a refuge from the office—it is a satellite office. Demands on modern families and other practicalities require people to take care of personal business during daytime hours, and work is often done after hours in the evening. Your people are accustomed to getting work done at home, and time in the office is not always spent on company business. With retirement funds an uncertain bet for the future, and pensions a thing of the past, many employees have or want to have a going business on the side. You can use this to your advantage to foster excellence, employing available technology and the ENHANCE performanceä model to embrace this new work ethic. We'll explore this further momentarily...

Your employees, regardless of generation or gender, will deliver value if you give them the flexibility they require to do it in a way that makes sense for them and your company. They will appreciate this respect and trust and will return the favor by working with diligence and care over the long haul. The lines between professional and personal life are blurred and rules are changing; social media and modern society have changed the way people relate to each other. One significant result that greatly impacts the workplace is the flattening of hierarchies; current expectations about access and perceptions of authority do not support trickle-down management and other established organizational structures that may be in place at your company. Today's employees do not blindly follow instructions; they need to understand and agree with what is required of them. Employees want to see the big picture and need you to connect the dots of how their job's responsibilities contribute to it. Moreover, today's employees value their time so much that they want to be more efficient, and are eager to help streamline your organization's operations. The more clearly you explain your overall objectives and goals, the better your employees will serve you—so long as you welcome and utilize their input.

How does all of this translate into practical steps you can take? Incorporate the characteristics below into your practices and policies; studies show they yield greater engagement. By doing this, you will successfully inspire today's talent to feel a sense of ownership. When your entrepreneurial employees feel like they have a personal stake in your company, they will give your company boundless effort and loyalty. Here are some simple tips derived from the ENHANCE performanceä model:

☐ **Mission-Driven Orientation and Continuous Context.** Employees want to know the big picture and see how they fit into it, in order get excited about their work and your company's initiatives and goals. Managers can incorporate this messaging into weekly staff meetings. If this is the sole purpose of your weekly staff meeting, that's finethe meeting will be short and perceived as helpful. This is absolutely necessary if you want your employees to give the extra time, thought, and energy that convert good into great. To be committed, today's employees want and need to care about your company, your customers, and the quality of what your organization delivers. Millennials are especially concerned about the impact their work will have on the world, and therefore how your company's purpose and goals will effect some kind of positive change. Use social media to provide messages on this point daily. Allow your millennial employees to do this on your company's behalf; provide training to fortify their ideas and enable them to use social media professionally and effectively.

☐ **Accountability and Integrity.** Those concepts are really two perspectives of the same picture. Your employees expect to see these practiced at all levels of the company, and will disengage if they see inconsistency between actions and stated values (particularly by management), a failure to provide visibility, or investments of resources that do not make sense based on business results or some other measure. Respect from your employees must be earned; it is no longer given according to rank or seniority. Integrity requires holding everyone, without exception, responsible to deliver what is promised to others inside and outside the company, as well as learning and doing what is needed and constantly improving. People are most engaged when they see admirable modeling, receive acknowledgement and recognition of their contribution, and see follow-up and specific, tangible or measurable outcomes as a result of their actions. This must be woven into the culture of your organization.

☐ **Alignment.** Employees are most engaged and committed when the goals or culture of your organization are aligned with their individual goals and values. Providing or allowing for flexible work arrangements can go a long way to achieve this. Managers should all be encouraged and empowered to sort out individual details with their team members. This component can also be achieved by using nuanced interviewing techniques to discover personal qualities, interests, and transferable skills, with less emphasis on previous job experience.

☐ **Communication.** This is the glue that holds your organization together (or poisons it, if done poorly). Thoughtful, open, honest, and respectful communication facilitates engagement. Without good communication practices, even the best strategic plans will fail. Poor communication disables execution and kills engagement. In order for your communications to be meaningful and effective, it is imperative that you inform your employees, but also solicit and respond to their feedback. This needs to be practiced by executives and managers, to model appropriate and desired communication. The company's internal website and communication tools should be available to employees and easy to navigate from anywhere, not just in the office, and fun to use. Setting this up or improving what exists can be a team building initiative that employees volunteer to participate in, an effort for which they should be recognized and rewarded. Use all available platforms and channels (email, social media, and meetings, as well as creative forums like corporate TV or internet radio, webinars, etc.) to seamlessly and openly communicate with your employees. For example, if you want to ensure IT folks receive a time-sensitive corporate communication, maybe texting or instant messaging during work hours is best. Also, providing all employees with a variety of communication-related training promotes acceptance of diversity, nonviolent communication, leadership, and other skills that will improve productivity.

☐ **Professional and Personal Development.** Organizations that are committed to training and developing employees' leadership and communications skills at all levels benefit from higher-performing workers in every area of the company. Not only does this improve overall performance and retention, it improves morale by demonstrating an interest in employees as people. This resonates with modern employees whose values prompt them to give back to those who help them. Additionally, better leadership skills and a shared language or style of communication promotes a cohesive culture and a sense of unity in diversity. This shared experience allows for internal mobility and alignment of interests, improving continuity and succession planning. Successful, established, and growing blue chip companies tend to promote from within and benefit from "lifers" who steadfastly provide their talents, tribal knowledge, and energy to the company's betterment. Your company's heritage depends on practices that foster continuity and retention.

Many of the methods and tools that enabled blue chip companies to retain employees 5, 10, 15+ years ago are no longer offered or no longer work, largely because the assumptions upon which they were based are no longer valid. For example, neither employees nor employers are promising "forever" when taking or offering a so-called permanent position. The incentives need to be different; they need to be short-term. Your employees are now asking your company the "What have you done for me lately?" question they had been accustomed to hearing from management. Plugging people into your organization like pegs in holes limits individual employees' contributions, ability to succeed, and continually provide value. It stifles their innovation and growth potential. Rigid job descriptions also limit your organization's flexibility and adaptability, while breaching its integrity. A Hudson study showed that one in five job descriptions do not accurately reflect the actual role and responsibilities of an employee in that job. That structure is intrinsically constrained and creates barriers to necessary change. Think about it: making up job descriptions and then looking for people who are an exact match—who have done that particular job already—is setting your organization up for obsolescence.

Do you really want to use a system that limits people's professional development, selects people who are less comfortable and skilled in dealing with change and stifles innovation? This time-honored method still works for certain groups, but generally it is not well adapted to today's dynamic work environment. When it is not working, you wind up simultaneously releasing and replacing people, devoting significant resources to reorganizing-constantly reinventing the wheel- instead of creating a better one with your team's talents and tribal knowledge. That trunk of history and miscellaneous inside information held by your employees is a treasure trove that will propel your organization forward if you just tap into it. But instead of investing in employees by developing them to take on new roles they have never done, this system has you cut them loose and starts from scratch with shiny new human resources who have "been there, done that" for somebody else already. Those people must then adapt to your company's unique way of doing things, and this transition of doing old things in new ways often leads to conflict and less productivity than expected.

Another common unintended consequence and symptom of this churn model is a "do-more-with-less" approach that sets employees up for failure. When change occurs in that environment, resistance, fear, and confusion ensues and productivity drops. This leaves your team just spinning its wheels thanks to a multitude of distractions. The standardized process of posting new job descriptions, "restructuring" to match people to them, and making big organizational announcements to explain the new *tactical approach de jour* based on a short-term view of a few people, is a broken model. There is a better way.

Employees are successfully attracted, motivated and retained with a simple model that profoundly improves performance and can be adapted to fit the needs of any organization. The ENHANCE performanceä model, outlined below, was designed to effect change and improve performance by addressing all of the factors that impact people's engagement.

Imagine being able to count on your team to improve the quality of your company's product or service and boost profitability, on their own initiative. Companies using this model have experienced improved performance, greater employee productivity and achieved up to 30 percent annual increases in revenue.

Here is an overview of the model:

Eliminate biases, distractions, pollutants, obstacles, and other barriers to productivity as much as possible. This includes providing programs and benefits that facilitate performance management.

Notice the strengths and weaknesses or your people, organizational model, team performance, and what causes and contributes to these advantages/

disadvantages and your organization's current results. This includes identifying all known obstacles, required resources, and any deficiencies in the team's composition and objectives. For example, is your team diverse enough to identify and represent the needs of your customers? This component gets everything out on the table and facilitates a culture that fosters brainstorming, collaboration and problem-solving.

Harness employees' input, skills and experience to create value, by capturing the full capabilities and potential of your team. This facilitates getting buy-in and teamwork. Tap your team members' collective knowledge and apply it to set the right goals, determine the best way to achieve them and successfully execute. Develop your team's skills and experience to continuously add value.

Align individual employees' based on common context/culture that promotes employees' interests and goals while meeting the needs and objectives of your company or your team and fostering Accountability. Ensure employees have a clear understanding of your company's big picture objectives, so they can stand behind and support that mission. Have an environment that allows team members to hold each other, and managers, accountable to deliver on their goals and responsibilities, including supporting everyone's individual success while helping the company reach its goals.

Navigate change and conflict by getting buy-in and fostering an environment of respect. Set expectations about how teams and individuals are expected to work together and validate these expectations are followed in practice. Adapt, improvise, and overcome with a culture that embraces flexibility.

Communicate daily (in some form) with your employees about the company's plans, both strategic and tactical. Highlight progress and achievements (including individual performance), but don't shy away from openly discussing challenges and setbacks. Be real. Build relationships by earning trust and respect, providing transparency, congruence, and consistency throughout the organization. This also helps ensure your organization's values, resources, and structures support individual and team efforts. Communication is key to setting people and your company up for success instead of delivering "Mission: Impossible" tasks.

Entrepreneurial execution and Evaluation of overall results. Regularly evaluating individual employee performance as well as your policies, structures, and practices. Involve your team in reviewing the company's performance and share the metrics with employees. Tweak strategies and tactics based on employees' suggestions, which fosters ownership. Provide opportunities for your employees to act as internal entrepreneurs to drive improvements that yield more profitability, quality and productivity for your organization.

The ENHANCE performance™ model can be plugged into any organization in a manner that provides maximum benefit by targeting areas of priority and need for improvement. Using this model will not only improve your company's performance, it will strengthen your corporate culture to consistently produce excellence, versatility and stewardship. Next, we explore the critical importance of culture to the profitability and future of your company.

Chapter 10

LEVERAGE CORPORATE CULTURE

Make Sure Your Foot Is On The Accelerator

We tend to think we can separate strategy from culture, but we fail to notice that in most organizations strategic thinking is deeply colored by tacit assumptions about who they are and what their mission is.

—EDGAR SCHEIN, MIT Sloan School of Management

THE ACHIEVEMENTS AND RESULTS your organization generates are a reflection of your team's culture. As stated by Harvard Business School professors John Kotter and James Heskett, the corporate culture can have a significant impact on your firm's long-term economic performance. Is yours the gas pedal or the brakes? Their research shows that organizational culture in fact dramatically moves the needle on financial results. A poignant exhibit from their book, *Corporate Culture and Performance*, underscores the value of cultural hygiene over time. By comparing twelve companies that had good cultural hygiene with twenty companies that did not maintain an emphasis on the integrity and quality of their culture, over an eleven-year period, they demonstrated that company culture generates real and measurable results (or consequences). See for yourself:

	Average Increase for Twelve Firms with Performance-Enhancing Cultures	Average Increase for Twenty Firms without Performance-Enhancing Cultures
Revenue Growth	682%	166%
Employment Growth	282%	36%
Stock Price Growth	901%	74%
Net Income Growth	756%	1%

Averages like these mean that some companies whose management did not maintain performance-enhancing cultures actually experienced losses. On the other hand, every company that invested in its culture reaped excellent returns as proven by the numbers.

Having a high-performance culture is key to your company's competitive advantage in the long run. Culture is the context and thrust that determines what gets produced, the quality of your products and services, and how people in your organization behave with each other, with vendors, and with customers. Your culture is unique; it is virtually impossible for others to copy. High-performing organizations create an environment with a distinct personality, a heart and soul, that sets a pace and passion for performance that inspires people to always do the right thing—go the extra mile to act in the best interest of the company. Implicit in this is the understanding that your culture will have weaknesses as well as strengths; being comprised of people, absolute perfection is not achievable. Strong teams are equally aware of their strengths and weaknesses—they know how to grow their strengths and address their weakness. Studies indicate that fewer than 10 percent of companies succeed in building a winning culture, and those that do often find it hard to maintain. However, the ENHANCE performance™ model provides a reliable framework to build, adapt, and maintain an extraordinary culture that fulfills your company's purpose.

Your company's culture is the collective, shared experience of your employees; it creates an identity with which they are associated. Everyone who interacts with your employees or your products and services recognizes that identity as a *brand*. As Tony Hsieh, CEO of Zappos, pronounced, "Your culture is your brand." Like branding and its marketing impact, culture shapes perceptions and sets the course for future outcomes. Since culture is so influential, employee engagement can help your organization only if it is built into and supported by your corporate culture. Culture is participatory and no single person or department owns the responsibility of creating, promoting, or fostering it.

Five factors contribute to a culture that is conducive to engagement, one in which employees are most likely to become truly committed and personally involved in their work. All of these factors are incorporated into the ENHANCE framework. At least some of these factors are imbedded in the daily processes, practices, and communications of the Fortune 500 companies (and others) consistently recognized by Forbes as "The Best Places to Work." Forbes derives its data from Glassdoor, where employees candidly share information about what it is like to work for their employers. There are a number of organizational characteristics that truly impact engagement levels:

☐ **Mission-driven orientation and ongoing context.** Employees want to know the big picture. They also need to understand how they fit into it, so they can get excited about their work and the company's initiatives and goals. Most importantly, this is what motivates employees to give that coveted "discretionary effort"—the extra time, thought and energy that elevates good to great. Employees need to care about your company, your customers, the quality of what you deliver to customers and the impact their work will have on the world by contributing to your goals.

☐ **Accountability and Integrity.** Those concepts are really just two sides of the same coin. This is a focus on business results and holding yourself and your departments, managers, and other individuals at all levels throughout the organization responsible for delivering what is needed to achieve stated goals and what is promised to others inside and outside the company. People are most engaged when they know there will be transparency, follow-up and tangible or measurable outcomes directly generated by their actions and performance.

☐ **Alignment.** Employees get most engaged when the goals and culture of your business are aligned with their individual goals or values. This is why engagement is relevant to employee acquisition and steers the hiring process towards the "right" employees—people who are a good and natural fit for your organization. This also requires acknowledging the need for flexibility and embracing the notion of work–life integration by implementing programs that set up mutually feasible work arrangements that maximize productivity and promote employee retention.

☐ **Communication.** This is the glue that holds everything together. Thoughtful communication with and among employees supports solid employee engagement. Without good communication practices, even the most well-intentioned, thoroughly evaluated strategic plans will fail. Poor communication kills engagement. Frequent, honest, clear, and respectful communication that informs, solicits, and responds to employee feedback is meaningful to employees. In order to create the possibility of employees being engaged, your company must facilitate information exchanges between its employees at all levels, so everyone can understand exactly how what they do at work every day affects the company's business goals and priorities.

☐ **Professional and Personal Development.** When organizations are committed to management training, leadership, and communications skills development and investing in their employees' professional growth and personal development, engagement, performance and retention levels go up and succession planning becomes possible. Blue Chip companies tend to promote from within and benefit from investing in developing their employees. Your company's success depends on the quality of the continuous development of your employees.

Incorporating these as elements of policies, practices, and work environment will boost the bottom line in both the short and long term. On the basis of its extensive 2013 employee engagement surveys, Gallup estimated that in the US alone, disengagement collectively costs companies a total of $450–$550 billion per year. Additionally, Gallup reports that the companies with the top 25 percent employee engagement scores are 22 percent more profitable than those in the bottom 25 percent with the lowest employee engagement levels. Companies cannot afford to stay in business with the costs caused by disengaged employees and the opportunities lost by failing to engage employees.

Even the most exalted, popular, and coveted companies today— such as Google, Facebook, and Apple—have kinks in their cultural armor. There is always room for growth and improvement. Diversity numbers that reveal gender and ethnic diversity imbalances are a clue about cultural shortcomings. Outmoded policies and practices that generate bad press, such as banning telecommuting, highlight areas for improvement.

Culture is the context that grabs people, so it is important to ensure your culture is a good fit for the types of people you want to attract and retain. Moreover, having a positive company-wide culture is critical to the overall strength of your company. Many companies with reputations as great places to work have pockets with holes—certain teams or departments that cannot keep employees because of a damaging subculture specific to that group. High turnover and poor team performance are signs of a management issue and cultural deficiency. Effective communications and daily interactions between management, employees, and peers, as well as department-to-department, reflect and shape the culture of an organization. Your company's culture is an integral component of its reputation, both internally and externally. Accordingly, sustaining success, growth, and innovation depends on the right culture. Your company culture is something to protect and invest in if you want to sustain teams that will support your goals and customers that will stay with you and sing your praises.

The ENHANCE model has all of the necessary ingredients to help you create and maintain an environment that's conducive to quality, innovation, and productivity. Following this model results in attracting and retaining teams that produce consistently positive outcomes. In order to sustain a high-performing culture, your organization must have these two primary characteristics, underpinned by the five components that follow:

✓ **Unique and recognizable.** Some companies, such as UPS, HSBC, and Varian, have a strong organizational personality—a "soul," if you will—derived from a deep heritage. Others, such as Southwest Airlines, Gap, and Google, create their own distinctive environment. This compelling combination of values, character, rituals, messages, and footprints creates a meaningful bond with employees, engaging them in their work because they find it inspiring and rewarding.

✓ **A set of commonly desired attitudes and behaviors among all employees and departments.** Lifting the hood to examine their distinctive corporate "personalities," you will find that they all encourage remarkably similar patterns of behavior. People in all of the organizations known for their great culture care passionately about quality and commercial success externally, while showing respect and concern for their colleagues internally. Employees think like owners, with an "action and results" orientation. They consistently build teamwork, emphasize professional and personal development, and are flexible and open to change. Integrity, accountability, and community are imbedded in their values.

These five components make an essential contribution to building and maintaining a strong culture:

1. A clear motivation and compelling "why"

2. Skills and knowledge that are not only acquired but also continually expanded and fine-tuned through personal and professional development opportunities and training.

3. Environment with policies, processes, and practices that reflect stated values and support success, diversity, innovation, and other factors that contribute to an adaptable, enduring culture

4. Structures and processes that facilitate social proof and reinforcement

5. Systems, benefits, and perks that provide acknowledgement and rewards to ensure loyalty and sustainability

The only businesses that will grow and sustain themselves today and in the future are the ones with leaders and managers driving cultures that support and promote the elements of employee engagement identified in this book. Culture is not just a set of values and policies, it is an environment of daily habits that amounts to a way of doing everything throughout your organization. Policies, procedures, tools and resources should be clear and consistent with each other and aligned with the goals of your company. The same applies to hiring procedures, employee benefits and perks, the physical work environment, and corporate events and programs. Everything about your company should project and reflect your cultural attributes —the culture that enables your company to achieve its objectives and underlies and informs your brand. This implies a need for accountability—tracking and measuring results—as well as a willingness to make adjustments. This does not mean you have to toss out everything and start from scratch. On the contrary, the most beneficial changes are often incremental adjustments based on feedback and lessons learned over time through experience. Culture, performance, and engagement are intertwined with effective leadership and management.

It goes without saying that your vision, mission, and style as a leader set the foundation for your company's culture, but a foundation is not a building nor is it a culture. Your leadership and management approach is key, but the actions of individual employees are equally important to establish and maintain a culture. Expression and execution of your strategically chosen culture requires your organization's leaders and managers to model the behaviors and values that define your company culture. Beneficial, results-driven cultures are carefully thought out and promulgated by leadership, not formulated as a consequence of the collective attitudes of the majority of employees. You can encourage desired actions and foster a desirable work ethic by noticing and acknowledging specific examples. Additionally, you should repeatedly clarify expectations and continuously mentor your employees. As a manager, you can help perpetuate the shared vision, mission, and goals by spreading the word through constant personal contact and communication with individual employees. Identify the influencers on your team, those who will buy in to the culture and whose words will carry weight with others. Be transparent and accessible, and be vigilant about preventing any breach of trust by holding yourself and all of your managers accountable for promoting employee engagement. Lack of trust is often the source of conflict, confusion, and unintended subcultures that undermine teamwork.

Culture defines the identity of your company, and people self-select based on whether or not they relate to what your company is about. For example, when I was an employee of a corporation with a reputation for being "cool, innovative, and disruptive" (in a good way), I noticed it attracted talented people who really cared about the company's mission, passionately worked long hours and were loyal advocates of the company. However, when I worked for a company whose employees were actively disengaged, there was constant discontent and poor execution, and none of management's strategies got fully implemented. That company also shrank and suffered severe financial losses. I have also worked for companies with accidental, undefined cultures and mixed levels of engagement, with certain departments performing better than others, which resulted in unsettling ups and downs, inconsistent quality, and unpredictable financial conditions. Of all of the companies I was with, only the company with a distinct, enduring culture had brand recognition and stood the test of time.

Why do engagement, diversity, and other culture-related strategies so often fail? Because these elements of organizational performance are not conducive to one-shot, quick fix solutions; they are not isolated issues that can be tackled by a single initiative, program, tiger team, or resource group. These are fundamental performance building blocks that require persistent, long-term, company-wide attention. No one person or department can oversee and manage a corporate culture. Every employee at every level has a role to play. Every employee wants a work culture that will allow them to continue to grow as a person, as well as serve as a secondary "home," since they are expected to devote so much time and energy to their job. Accordingly, work should be personally enriching. In a 2012 study conducted by MTV, nine out of ten respondents (representing your current and future employee candidates) said that a "social and fun" workplace is an important factor when selecting a job. Further, 83 percent of respondents stated that they are "looking for a job where their creativity is valued." Employees themselves play a major role in making that possible. A high-performance culture captures all that enthusiasm and develops and channels it professionally and productively.

Here are some specific examples of how the ENHANCE performance™ model has been applied to shore up company cultures, increase engagement, and boost revenues. Try them in your organization!

Eliminated barriers to productivity and diversity

1. Implemented a flexible work environment. Flexibility in the workplace ranks as the most important incentive, following cash and health benefits, to all generations and addresses impediments to having a diverse workforce. Introduced remote office model, in which employees were given tools and access to corporate resources via computer from any location. In this case, the IT department used standard company hardware and software to set up remote access, based on functionality available in the current Microsoft operating system.

This approach included a communication plan for remote employees:

2. Managers and employees reserved a specific time each day or week to meet virtually, and these sessions were treated as if they were face-to-face meetings by silencing devices and removing all distractions. (GoToMeeting and Skype are popular platforms for conducting virtual meetings.)

3. Offered communication workshops and training for all employees on elimination of bias to support diversity and workplace civility, as well as develop healthy conflict management skills.

4. Provided certain "life services," based on employee input, to minimize time spent running necessary errands and distractions caused by time-related worries.

5. Introduced tools for managing and monitoring remote employees, which are only used transparently (that is, employees know they are being tracked and how) for certain functions. Some specific software tools I recommend are included in the Appendix.

Noticed strengths and weaknesses

1. Instituted periodic HR-facilitated meetings for all departments and functions, including executive staff, to acknowledge successes, identify areas for improvement, brainstorm, conduct post-mortems on project delays and missed targets, and evaluate ideas for future growth.

2. Provided train the facilitator workshop to HR and managers, to develop their skills for professional, organized meeting facilitation to ensure meetings are productive, meaningful and actionable.

Harnessed team expertise and perspectives to improve performance

1. Incorporated "reverse mentoring" technique to ensure all team members were heard.

2. Facilitated team meetings for specific projects to expedite consensus on solutions to identified issues and agree on roles, responsibilities, and dependencies within the team.

3. Drove consistent adoption of changes, in part by utilizing the RACI matrix to capture and share what was agreed upon by the team, and coaching managers to implement accountability-based follow up on action items.

Aligned interests and Accountability

1. Offered instant rewards (gift cards of varying values under $100.00) in recognition of exemplary effort, offering helpful ideas, or otherwise taking initiative and putting forth extra effort.

2. Established that managers were required to perform a one-on-one each month dedicated to checking in on how employees are feeling about their work, the company, and their career plans.

3. Weekly huddles between managers and their team as a group, as well as individually, to foster communication, accountability and alignment.

Navigated changes in response to company growth

1. Established goal-setting performed on a quarterly basis as an interactive exercise between the manager and employees. Employees were encouraged to express their professional goals and interests and feedback on performance was provided (performance coaching—no ratings), expectations were clearly communicated and validated with the employee and opportunities or needs for professional development and training were identified, along with an action plan for pursuing it. This promoted retention and improved productivity in the face of organizational changes and restructuring of positions.

2. Held facilitated meetings to get input from employees about existing processes, gaps, resource needs and suggested improvements, and then decide which suggestions to implement.

3. Managers communicated decisions and reasoning behind changes made and ideas not implemented.

Communicated the mission

1. Worked with company's marketing group to create an infographic to display the company's mission, vision, history, and values. This was posted around the office as well as on the company's website.

2. Instituted beginning every all-hands meeting with a brief recitation of the company vision and mission by the CEO.

3. Managers incorporated a discussion of company values into all staff meetings, one-on-ones, and team-building events, in a variety of entertaining ways (icebreakers, corporate "war stories," games and competitions among the team for exhibiting corporate values, etc.).

4. Instituted providing daily messages reinforcing the company's mission, in a variety of electronic and paper formats, delivered directly to all employees and posted on the company intranet.

Executed policies and processes to drive and evaluate results

1. Retooled headcount to be more fluid between organizations and provide opportunities for employees to fashion their own jobs based on identified needs and individual skills, interest, and potential

2. Revised onboarding processes to ensure a true dialogue around priorities, goals, expectations, and work preferences

3. Instituted ways to measure and publicize incremental team successes

4. Implemented team calendars to streamline team communications and provide greater visibility of efforts and progress

5. Performed stay interviews to discover why people were with the company

6. Conducted surveys to identify inter-departmental performance issues and established initiatives to implement solutions

The key takeaway for you is that a desirable corporate culture is not a luxury—it is a necessity. The impacts of your culture on your organizational performance are quantifiable. Developing a specific culture is practical and relevant for organizations of every size and stage of development, including (indeed, *especially*) start-ups. Your organization's culture is an evolving appliance that either supports or undermines the success of all your efforts and goals. Using the ENHANCE model demystifies the concept of corporate culture by breaking it down into an actionable pieces that translate into a performance plan for your organization. Next, let's take a look at how you can measure the effectiveness of your culture at propelling performance to new levels.

Chapter 11

READING THE GAUGES RIGHT

Measuring The Success Of Your Culture And Employee Engagement

The bottom line is down where it belongs—at the bottom. Way above it in impor-
tance are the infinite number of events that produce the profit or the loss.

—PAUL HAWKEN, *Growing a Business*

WOULD YOU DRIVE THE car you are selling? Ask yourself this question about your company, as well as the products or services it offers- would you buy it or its offerings? If your honest response is hesitant or not completely affirmative, that is an informative gauge of employee engagement and your company's culture. The value your business delivers to customers, owners, shareholders, and employees is the only meaningful metric of employee engagement. For publicly traded companies, stock price is more than a measure of financial performance—it is an assessment of your corporate culture's social validity. Your stock price acts as proof of your company's value and an indicator of your employees' level of engagement. Profitability and stock valuation are concrete indicators of how well your employee engagement efforts and your corporate culture are serving your strategic objectives.

The latest research on the impact of employee engagement shows that companies named in the "100 Best Companies to Work For" list published annually in *Fortune* also perform best in the stock market. A July 2014 report jointly produced by the Wharton School and the Warwick Business School revealed that American companies that invest in their people and are regarded as being good to their employees are rewarded with 2–3 percent better annual returns in the stock market than competitors who did not make the best employer list. The "100 Best Companies to Work For" list garners widespread attention from investors, shareholders, management, employees, and the media, and is now compiled for companies based in more than forty-five countries around the world. The influence of this all-star list dramatically demonstrates that employee engagement and corporate culture are valuable assets. A reliable, straightforward way to measure the success of your company's efforts to build and maintain a high performance culture is to simply look at the market, (your market share and acquisition prospects if you are private) and your company's profits. Investor attention and the studies findings justify and support budgeting to increase employee engagement; they also advocate the wisdom of investing in building a robust and unique corporate culture.

The positive press and high regard attached to the best-place-to-work designation establishes a company's reputation and serves as a valuable tool for recruitment, retention, and motivation in competitive labor markets. The top 100 places to work score is based on a survey of 250 employees randomly selected from each company in the running, and an evaluation of each candidate organization on the following factors:

✓ demographic makeup

✓ pay and benefits programs

✓ corporate culture

Companies are scored in four areas:

1. Credibility, based on communications and interactions with employees

2. Respect for employees, based on professional development opportunities and benefits

3. Fairness, based on compensation and diversity

4. Pride and camaraderie, based on teamwork, philanthropy, and celebrations each company promotes and sponsors

Collectively, a "great place to work" is defined as a place in which "you can trust people you work for, have pride in what you do, and enjoy the people you work with."

Some companies ranked among the top ten on this list even outperformed the stock market. For example, Google stock was up more than 32 percent compared to a 15 percent return on the S&P 500 in the same year. This further boosts excitement about the company among its employees (and potential employees). Nevertheless, Google still has room for improvement, based on its published diversity statistics and word on the street about certain workgroups within Google that are anomalies to its otherwise enticing culture. Of course engagement and culture are not the sole reasons for these companies' high stock prices, but engaged, productive employees are the foundation of the products and services that drive value.

The overwhelming feedback linking things like "employee satisfaction," "happy employees," and "engaged employees" to higher levels of profitability and market value acknowledges and underscores the fact that nothing happens without the efforts of the people inside the companies. Clearly, everyone in your organization has a direct impact on your company's culture and the degree to which your people are engaged in their work and performing optimally. The recognition that employees play such a profound role in a company's success or failure puts a different twist on Milton Friedman's classic view that a corporation's "only concern is to use its resources and engage in activities designed to increase its profits." In the modern business environment, this means a corporation's primary concern must be for its employees because investing in *human* resources enables the company to engage in activities that will increase profits. Modern business case studies, like those surveyed in *Built to Last* and *Great by Choice*, show that companies with consistent focus on building and maintaining strong and clearly defined corporate cultures outperformed others by at least ten times.

The ENHANCE model incorporates all of the determinants of a great place to work. It plugs the gaps in your organization's existing culture to generate measurable results in the broadly accepted employee engagement and performance-culture indicators. Having an accurate way of gauging the performance of your culture not only helps you determine ROI, it is necessary for maintaining and improving performance and increasing your bottom line. The challenge is that the culture and engagement measurement methods and tools sometimes used by HR professionals are generic, complicated, distracting to employees, and biased (subject to widely varying application and interpretation). They do not provide an accurate assessment of engagement levels or cultural impact, nor do they provide actionable information. Instead, try using simple tools and methods that focus on evaluating your employees' knowledge and understanding of your brand, messaging, and core values—including an ability to articulate your vision and mission statement in their own words. Another worthwhile measurement objective would be an analysis of your organization's actual culture. It is critical to determine your baseline culture and its ability to promote a uniform, distinct value set that is reflected throughout the company, as well as validate whether or not your intended culture is in practice.

A well-designed cultural assessment will identify individual, team, or corporate objectives, assumptions, attitudes, policies and practices that are inconsistent with company values. Engagement assessments should explore the quality and quantity of leadership; teamwork; adaptability; collaboration; openness; communication; diversity; and commitment that exists within your organization. Assessments are best used as guide posts to indicate weaknesses and strengths. It is unrealistic to expect any internal measurement to provide a reliable score of your team's engagement or culture—your company's profits, valuation in the market, and public reputation ultimately do that. View the internal measurements by HR as the fuel gauge in your car: you need this information to take appropriate actions to course correct and adjust performance, but only your company's results in the marketplace and ability to retain and attract great employees provides the true rating of your organization's culture and success at engaging employees.

Create a "culture gauge" that enables you to see at a glance how much fuel is in your tank. Having noted this basic marker, you can drill down into the details to determine why the needle on your gauge is pegging in the yellow or red zones. Anonymous testing and data collection in a relaxed, comfortable environment is key to obtaining candid and accurate results. Here are the key areas to include on your culture gauge:

- ☐ **Knowledge** – Do employees know what your corporate values are, and can they recognize behavior and decision making that is consistent (or inconsistent) with those values?

- ☐ **Perceptions** – Opinions about what values are actually being practiced and exemplified. Gather employees' independent, detailed descriptions of your company culture. Questions should focus on identifying what the real values and priorities are in day-to-day operations and interactions versus what is stated in value statements and policies. For example, a lot of companies talk about diversity, but tend to hire people that look and think alike and who went to the handful of universities where they always do their recruiting. Here's another: one-word values, like *communication,* may be listed as corporate values, but what does that mean to your employees? And what does communication look like within your organization; is it open and transparent, or inconsistent and ambiguous?

- ☐ **Behavior** – Collect examples of good and bad decisions made by employees, as well as employees' actions that align with your company values (or don't). Do you have employees who dress inappropriately or interact poorly with others? Track how often employees take initiative or make judgment calls with results that were beneficial. If one of your values is work–life balance, you might measure how many employees work while they are on vacation or how much vacation your employees take and what team or organizational dynamics may be impeding them. If your value is accountability, you might track how many employees are disciplined or fired for poor performance.

It is also important to measure your culture at least once a quarter to catch fluctuations. Annual metrics on any aspect of performance is useless because things change more quickly than that, and corrections are best made in a timely manner if they are to be meaningful and effective. Finally, aggregate the results of employee actions to show their impact on your company's bottom line. For example, any cost savings realized by specific employee actions should be tracked and tallied. These data points can then be shared throughout the organization. These measurement methods also facilitate recognition/award programs.

Different functions have a role to play in evaluating the effectiveness of engagement efforts and ensuring the perpetuation of a high-performance culture. Your employees must all understand and exemplify the corporate values in a consistent manner. Additionally, everyone in your company needs to take responsibility for their own engagement through career management: seeking or creating opportunities within your company and initiating a dialogue with their managers. Managers should be tasked with the day-to-day, quarterly and annual exercises required to collect the pertinent data. HR must provide the guidance, structures, policies, processes, and tools that managers need, with support from finance, IT, executives, and legal. Executives are tasked with generating enthusiasm about the company's vision and mission. Further, they set the strategic culture, modeling and enforcing it and staying tuned in to the market's reaction to keep score based on the company's bottom-line.

Now let's take a look at some real-world examples that tie this all together and drive it home...

Chapter 12

MAINTAINING THE CHASSIS

Connecting All The Parts For High Performance

A group of people get together and exist as an institution we call a company so they are able to accomplish something collectively that they could not accomplish separately—they make a contribution to society, a phrase which sounds trite but is fundamental.

—DAVID PACKARD, co-founder of Hewlett-Packard

IF YOU ARE NOT engaging your employees as part of a productive culture, your company will languish, struggle, and ultimately fade away. Companies drive growth by empowering employees to take chances and try new ways of doing things. When organizations successfully engage their customers and their employees, they receive 240 percent greater performance-based results, according to Blessing and White's research, compared to companies with neither engaged employees nor engaged customers.

The real point of employee engagement is to foster a culture of teamwork to accomplish great things and to provide solid financial returns. The key to engaging employees is understanding what they want, and need, and giving it to them in a way that aligns their interests with yours. Executive leaders and people managers are to employees what marketing and sales reps are to customers. Corporate leaders in the C-suite need to model the character of your company, and managers need to follow suit and spread the message, exemplify it, and coach and mentor your employees to do the same. Managers bear the responsibility of connecting the dots between what employees do and the bigger corporate picture, so that even employees who never interact directly with customers know their work is vital to the company's mission and vision. Managers are instrumental in encouraging employees to feel good about their contribution to the company's well-being. HR's role is to provide the guidance, tools, and support that managers and executives need to successfully engage employees and provide the right cultural context.

Collaborative high performance is the essence of teamwork. Your organization will stumble unless you focus on leveraging your team's best ideas and full set of skills to achieve your goals. Pollutants and barriers—like mismanaged conflicts, workplace bullying, and distractions caused by inadequate support or rewards—undermine attention to goals and the achievement of them.

The companies that stand the test of time are those that create an environment that's conducive to building relationships and getting results. They constantly strive for improvement, implement changes, and make decisions based on employee input backed by solid metrics. They also continue to adapt, grow, and expand. Setbacks are a reality every organization must confront at some point, a test that can be taken in stride if your company has a clear and compelling set of values to which its leaders adhere. As a leader, you are responsible for aligning your people with your corporate culture. It's up to you to rally them and encourage them to embrace an inspiring mission that will collectively propel you into the future. Having the right cultural imperatives and never compromising them will prepare your organization to drive safely through any storm.

Engage, respect, and trust your employees, and sustained success will follow.

Many successful businesses are now focusing on creating family-friendly programs and a company culture that allows for diversity and better work–life balance, including flexible schedules and generous family leave policies.

Let's review a few examples. These Fortune 500 companies have been included in *Working Mother* magazine's "100 Best Companies." *Working Mother* looks for companies with family-friendly benefits (such as paid maternity leave), flexible cultures that enable employees to have dinner at home with their kids, and benefits that allow working moms to advance. The survey also highlights the number of women in the C-suite.

Verizon Communications

In 2012, Verizon debuted "Mobility at Work," a program that makes dedicated office space available to the growing number of employees who aren't tethered to a specific location. Seventy-six percent of its employees now telecommute and the company is testing a work from home pilot program. Certain locations have on-site child care or access to up to ten days of subsidized backup care annually. Also, child care necessitated by business-related travel may be reimbursed up to $80 per day.

Women managers/execs – 32 percent

Unilever

Achieving gender balance is a priority for all top-level executives at this company. Unilever also promotes inclusiveness through its Global Diversity Board and maintains a formal mentoring initiative to facilitate promoting high-potential female talent. The company also has a Women's Interactive Network that offers professional development programs.

Women managers/execs – 40 percent

Women hires in 2012 – 56 percent

Women employees – 43 percent

Employees who use a flextime schedule – 39 percent

Employees who telecommute – 48 percent

Genentech

Genentech highlights near-site day care facilities offering priority enrollment and affordable backup care. Employees are reimbursed up to $250 annually to cover additional child-care expenses. In Arizona, Oregon, and New Mexico, manufacturing workers can access home-based child care. Expectant parents can sign up for "Having a Baby" classes that shows them how to maximize their leaves and benefits. Full-time employees with seven years' tenure get paid sabbaticals.

Women managers/execs – 17 percent

Microsoft

Parents can take up to twelve weeks of leave to care for a newborn, newly adopted or recently placed foster child. The employee has twelve months from the birth of the child/placement in the home to take the leave. If the leave is taken within the first six months of the birth, the first four weeks of this leave are paid at 100 percent of base salary. Birth mothers may take up to eight weeks of paid leave at 100 percent of base salary. Monthly classes on a variety of topics geared for new and expecting parents are provided on-site. Microsoft arranges for discounts on day-care tuition and backup child care. The company also provides private "New Mothers Rooms" for breast-feeding and milk storage. A dedicated leave of absence program manager assists employees with questions and arranges consultation on topics such as child care, child development, and special-needs children.

Flex Scheduling: All employees, including new parents, have the opportunity to work from home or remotely and create a flexible schedule. Job sharing is also an option.

Aflac Insurance

This company offers amenities such as a lactation room for new mothers, pre- and post-adoption placement counseling, and an on-site resource center that gives employees access to information on work and family issues. Aflac offers the largest on-site child-care facility in Georgia and provides extended between the hours of 5:30 a.m. and 11:30 p.m. The center provides certified and experienced caregivers and serves more than 600 children. It features an open-door policy for parents to visit during the work day; a pre-K program; transportation to and from school for school-aged children; and an after-school program including dance, gymnastics, and arts and crafts. Aflac sports a workforce comprising 70 percent women, of which approximately 70 percent are mothers. More than 51 percent of the company's supervisors are women with children, and the proportion of female VPs and executives combined is 30 percent.

American Express

American Express provides free access to work–life personal assistants who can locate reputable child-care centers, contractors, lawyers, tutors, and more. The company boasts sixteen employee networks for professional guidance, including such hot topics as virtual workers, women in technology, and millennials. Employees can also access online educational sessions and discussions about the challenges of caring for elder parents or relatives with special needs. There are also programs for families dealing with autism, diabetes, cancer, and migraines; free private counseling is also available.

Women employees – 63 percent

Women managers – 46 percent

"The only thing of real importance that leaders do is to create and manage culture." "If you do not manage culture, it manages you, and you may not even be aware of the extent to which this is happening."

—EDGAR SCHEIN, professor MIT Sloan School of Management

It is essential to create a culture designed to attract, motivate, and retain people with the talents and mindset needed to achieve your organization's goals. Wherever there is a gathering of people, a culture of some sort emerges. It is easier and more fruitful to manage a culture created by design, with a goal or purpose in mind, than to rein in an "accidental" culture. In the absence of a positive and coherent culture that is carefully nurtured and steadfastly guarded, individuals at any level of your organization can, intentionally or otherwise, hijack your team and redirect or stymie its efforts. Examples can be found in almost any company, regardless of size—even companies with strong cultures that breed success. However, organizations that take pride in their culture actively seek to identify and resolve discordance. A predetermined culture serves as a compass for your organization; it guides hiring decisions, attracts compatible talent, facilitates cohesiveness and diversity (because values like quality, innovation, and integrity transcend bias), and promotes commitment and communication.

Culture-driven team building puts an emphasis on identifying individuals' core qualities; with a strong culture as a foundation, you can confidently allow your team members the freedom to meet specific objectives in the way they see fit. When you are working within a definitive culture to which everyone is committed, traditional job descriptions and subversive politics become unnecessary. Instead, roles and responsibilities can be assigned based on ability, knowledge, expertise, and interest. When an individual's role is determined in a transparent and merit-based manner it is naturally respected by everyone. Previous job experience becomes tangential; the only experience that really matters—and actually moves the needle—is the experience gained on the job as applied to your particular objectives. Transferable skills and attitude prove to be more important than "industry experience." Organizational plans, technology, and market conditions change rapidly; previous experience doing the "same" type of work quickly becomes outdated and virtually obsolete. To be competitive, an employee must stand out by offering something unique or of extraordinary value to your market. Your team's efforts will inherently be innovative to some degree. As a result, an employee's demonstrated ability to adapt to change is often a more relevant predictor of value to your organization. Flexible employees are creatively nimble and naturally make greater contributions within a more dynamic environment.

Corning's challenging foray into fiber optics offers a classic example of how corporate culture comes into play when a company is faced with major disruptive change. The amazing metamorphosis from the Corning Glass Works (founded in 1851) into a multinational high-tech materials corporation exemplifies the principles and rewards of an employee-focused culture as discussed throughout this book. Thanks to well-defined values of innovation, inclusion/diversity, resourcefulness, persistence, and integrity, Corning's leaders were able to turn to their employees when the company needed to embrace a radical change of direction. Employees with no previous experience in fiber optics recognized the need for Corning to repurpose its existing workforce and equipment to tap this promising new market segment. Management trusted its front-line employees and the team delivered in spades. Corning continually strives to improve and adapt, and despite the occasional missteps, which are to be expected, Corning owes its long tenure to its solid corporate culture that incorporates a commitment to accountability and excellence.

To find more examples, you need look no further than *Fortune's* annual "100 Best Companies to Work For" list. All of these companies demonstrate the awareness that today's business environment requires your company to be nimble without compromising stability and soul. The blueprint for a high-performance business vehicle is represented by the following formula:

(Respectful Leadership + Coaching and Mentoring)

X

(Strong ENHANCE Model Culture Supporting Employee Engagement)

= Future Proof Company

The real point of employee engagement is to foster a culture of teamwork to accomplish great things and to provide solid financial returns.

We've laid out the fundamentals of engaging employees to cultivate more high performers who will help you build and sustain a successful company. We've synthesized and summarized extensive research by notable companies and organizations to provide you with instructive information to help guide your HR strategies in acquiring, motivating, and retaining ideal employees. Data from reliable surveys provided greater insight about modern employees' expectations, work ethic, and attitudes, as well as the consequences of failing to address them properly. Examples of how prominent companies have successfully engaged employees and used their culture to survive and thrive demonstrated the competitive advantages of adapting to change and affording employees the flexibility to thrive personally as well as professionally. Here are the key themes:

✓ Employees will only contribute value in proportion to the support you give them.

✓ Great, high-performing, engaged employees are nurtured, not found.

**Oh and, as the sagacious detective Columbo used to say,
"There's just one more thing..."
And it's a big, hairy, smoking gun kind of thing.**

Millennials and the new generation entering the workforce in a few years (Gen Z) are demanding acknowledgement of their value and human dignity from employers, *as well as the companies they invest in and buy from.* Consequently, now more than ever, your company is only as good as your employees *and your reputation with them*—social media and the Internet have empowered employees to influence customers and investors. Inspire employees with opportunities to better themselves and the world, and they will over-deliver by being loyal ambassadors of your company and its offerings, as well as superstar employees. A number of Gen Xers and the majority of millennials favor socially responsible investments. As a result, socially responsible investing is on the rise—and investors and fund managers are taking heed. Socially responsible investments (SRI) are not limited to solar and other obviously "green" investments. The strategy of SRI is wide-reaching: to encourage and support corporations that consider both financial returns and social good. Investors and funds focused on SRI look for corporate practices or products that promote environmental stewardship, consumer protection, human rights, and diversity. The impression you make on your employees now has far-reaching impacts, and will directly impact your stock price and company valuation.

Technology has given this new crop of idealists, who want to change the world, the means to express their values for financial gain and drive them with economic power. The majority of millennials are entrepreneurial types, and early indications are that Gen Z is even more so; many will not want to work for someone in the absence of aligned values and an ability to maintain their desired lifestyle. Combine this with the fact that Gen Xers and millennials are set up to inherit forty-one <u>trillion</u> dollars from boomers over the next forty years, according to the World Economic Forum report, and consider the leverage your workforce will have—they will have the inclination, and the means, to walk away from a job with your company if it is undesirable in any way. To attract and retain good talent, you'll need to provide flexibility and compelling, meaningful reasons to stay. The pool of employees is going to dramatically shrink in the coming decades.

So you think it is competitive to find and attract talent now? It is only going to get tougher, and the time to prepare for what is coming started *yesterday.* Some companies are already making strides to entice employees to stay and new talent to join their teams, and even those companies have more work to do. However, they have a jump on the competition, and those that are quick to adopt the principles we've outlined here, will as well. Don't let your company get left behind; take action today to ENHANCE employee engagement!

On a final note, in this book I endeavored to provide practical guidance, a framework, and actionable information, reinforced by decades of my own experience and the research findings of others. My hope is that you found this to be a valuable resource you will use and share with others. If you found this book helpful and would like more information, visit

www.employeeandclientengagement.com

APPENDIX A

Remote Employee Monitoring Software

---

1. Hivedesk Good for multiple remote workers on multiple projects: Workers check in by identifying their project from the central hub and Hivedesk tracks their time and adds each day's information to the weekly time sheet.

Hivedesk snaps random screenshots so you know what your employee has up on their screen and it also sends a graphical productivity gauge for each worker.

Compatible with Windows, Mac and Linux. Fee based service.

2. Worksnaps If you need more detail, this takes screenshots every 10 minutes and logs keyboard strokes and mouse movement. In addition, it catalogs applications that were used so you can tell how much time an employee spent reading a Word document or working in an Excel spreadsheet.

Gives managers access to reports and has an optional webcam feature that allows you to see not just what's on a worker's screen but the worker as well.

Compatible with Windows, Mac and Linux. Fee based.

REFERENCES

Chapter 1

1. Gallup's State of the American Workplace report, 2013. (findings from 2010-2012)

2. Blessing White's 2013 Employee Engagement Research Report (January 2013)

3. Gallup's State of the American Workplace report, 2010. (findings from 2008-2010)

4. "Closing the Engagement Gap: A Road Map for Driving Superior Business Performance" Global Workforce Study (2007-2008). Towers Perrin.

Chapter 2

1. "Diversity as an Engine of Innovation." Deloitte Review Issue 8 (2011) Deloitte Development LLC

2. "Moving Mind-sets on Gender Diversity" McKinsey Global Survey results (2013)

3. McKinsey & Company. (2007). "Women matter: Gender diversity, a corporate business driver. "

4. US Census Bureau, 2012 Projections. White people will no longer be majority of American population in the US by 2043, no single racial or ethnic group will constitute a majority of the US population

Chapter 3

1. Gallup's State of the American Workplace report, 2010. (findings from 2008-2010)

2. Watson Wyatt WorkUSA Study (2002). Watson Wyatt's 2008/2009 WorkUSA Report found that when employees are highly engaged, their companies enjoy 26 percent higher employee productivity, and those companies earned 13 percent greater total returns to shareholders over the last five years. Additionally, highly engaged employees are twice as likely as their less engaged peers to be top performers. Engaged employees miss 20% fewer days of work and tend to be more supportive of organizational change initiatives.

3. *Industrial and Labor Relations Review* (2012); employees with the highest levels of commitment (using the same definition as "engagement" in this book) perform 20 percent better and are 87 percent less likely to leave an organization.

Chapter 4

1. "The Future of Eating: Who's Eating What in 2018?" (2014) The NPD Group

2. "Meet Generation Z: Forget Everything You Learned About Millennials" (2014) by Sparks & Honey, marketing agency.

3. "The Millennial Mind Goes to Work: How Millennial Preferences Will Shape the Future of the Modern Workplace." (2013) Bentley University study report

4. *PwC's "NextGen: A global generational study" (2013)*

Chapter 5

1. HR Solutions Inc., employee engagement surveys (2014)

2. Gallup *2013 State of the American Workplace* report

3. Blessing White's 2013 Employee Engagement research report

4. Chapter 6

5. The Workplace Bullying & Trauma Institute (WBTI), 2003 Report on Abusive Workplaces; by Gary Namie, Ph.D.; October, 2003.

6. Harrison Psychological Associates; Workplace bullying's high cost: $180M in lost time, productivity; Orlando Business Journal - March 15, 2002 by Liz Urbanski Farrell; March 2002

7. The Workplace Bullying Institute (WBI), Report on 2013 Workplace Bullying Survey; by Gary Namie, Ph.D..

8. The Lindenberger Group LLC, Workplace Bullying Survey (2012)

9. UMIST - Destructive Conflict and Bullying at Work, Sponsored by the British Occupational Health Research Foundation (BOHRF); By Helge Hoel & Cary L Cooper; Manchester School of Management; April 2000.

10. Bullying in the Workplace; by Canada's Safety Council; September 2000; http://www.safety-council.org/info/OSH/bullies.html

Chapter 7

1. The 2013 Culture and Change Management Survey. Strategy& Formerly Booz and Company (www.strategyand.pwc.com)

2. Culture's Role in Enabling Organizational Change (2013) by DeAnne Aguirre director of the Katzenbach Center and partner Strategy&, Formerly Booz and Company (www.strategyand.pwc.com)

Chapter 8

1. Gallup *2013 State of the American Workplace* report

2. "Attracting and Retaining High-Technology Talent," co-sponsored by William M. Mercer, Inc. and the Pittsburgh High Technology Council

3. "Latest Telecommuting Statistics" GlobalWorkplaceAnalytics.com 2013

Chapter 9

1. Hudson .com staffing agency study 2013

Chapter 10

1. The 2013 Culture and Change Management Survey. Strategy& Formerly Booz and Company (www.strategyand.pwc.com)

2. "No Collar Workers" a MTV 2012

Chapter 11

1. "Employee Satisfaction, Labor Market Flexibility, and Stock Returns Around The World" by Alex Edmans, Lucius Li, Chendi Zhang(July 2014) **NBER Working Paper No. 20300** (jointly produced by the Wharton School and the Warwick Business School)

Chapter 12

1. "From the Margins to the Mainstream: Assessment of the Impact Investment Sector and Opportunities to Engage Mainstream Investors" A **2012-2014 report by the World Economic Forum Investors Industries** Prepared in collaboration with Deloitte Touche Tohmatsu

INDEX

F

Facebook, 117
facilitators, of brainstorming sessions, 48
fairness, *Fortune's* selection criteria, 127
family-friendly programs, 133–135
fear and change management, 87, 92–93
firings. *See* layoffs and termination
flexible work arrangements
    cost savings due to, 100–101
    electronic tracking of remote employees, 122, 141
    engagement and, 72
    in ENHANCE performance™ model, 104–106, 107, 121–122
    Gallup surveys on remote employees, 72
    GlobalWorkplaceAnalytics on remote employees, 100
Forbes, Malcolm, 31
Forbes, The Best Companies To Work For In 2014, 34, 115
Fortune, 100 Best Companies to Work For, 125–127, 137
Fortune 500 companies, 33, 100, 115, 133–135
    See also specific companies
Frankel, Barbara, 82
Friedman, Milton, 127

G

Gallup surveys
    on employee attitudes and performance, 98–99
    on employee commitment, 46
    on employee engagement, 46
    on lost productivity in US, 24, 117
    on profitability and employee engagement, 68, 117
    on profitability and gender diversity, 34–35
    on ratio of employee disengagement, 25
    on remote employees, 72
Gap, 118
gender and workplace bullying, 78, 79–80
gender diversity and profitability, 32, 34–35
Genentech, 134

generational groups, viewpoints of, 51–64
    alignment among, 54, 62
    apprenticeships, 61
    authority, 56–57
    educational debt, 59
    entrepreneurship, 59, 104–106, 139
    loyalty, 64
    mobile work flexibility, 61
    money, 57, 58
    motivational phrases, 62–63
    multi-generational best practices, 61–64
    rewards, 62–63
    short-term incentives, 62
    technology, 56, 58
    two-way mentoring, 61–62
    volunteerism, 59
    work-life balance, 57
    See also specific groups
Gen X, 53, 55–56, 57–58, 59, 60, 61–62, 63, 139
Gen Y, 15, 53, 56–57, 59, 60–62, 63, 64, 72, 104–105, 107, 138, 139
Gen Z, 15, 54, 56, 59, 61, 105, 138, 139
Glassdoor, 26, 115
Global Diversity Board (Unilever), 133
GlobalWorkplaceAnalytics, on remote employees (2013), 100
Google, 117, 118, 127
GoToMeeting, 121
Great by Choice (Collins and Hansen), 128
group meals, 47

H

Hawken, Paul, 125
Heskett, James, 113–114, *114*
high-performance companies, 131–139
    success formula for, 137
    Aflac Insurance, 135
    American Express, 135
    Genentech, 134
    Microsoft, 134
    Unilever, 133–134
    Verizon Communications, 133
Hivedesk (software), 141

HR Solutions Inc., study on employee dissatisfaction (2014), 67

HSBC, 118

Hsieh, Tony, 115

Hudson Highland Group, on accuracy of job descriptions, 109

human resources departments (HR)
  inclusive approach to organizational change, 91
  measurement methods and tools of, 128
  periodic meetings to notice strengths and weaknesses, 122
  role of, 14, 24, 44, 69–70, 132
  workplace bullying policies, 80–81, 86

I

incentives, 62, 99, 100, 109

Industrial and Labor Relations Review, on employee commitment (2012), 46

insurance costs, 79

integrity
  ENHANCE performance™ model, 107, 111, 115–116

Internships.com, study on Gen Z, 59

interpersonal conflict, 26, 37, 73

interviews, 84, 97, 107, 124

investment in companies, 125–130

investment in employees, 23–25, 47, 64, 71, 126–128

J

job descriptions, 104, 109

K

Karr, Jean-Baptiste Alphonse, 59

Katzenbach Center, on change management, 90–91

Kenexa, on profitability of engaged companies, 28

knowledge, in cultural gauge, 129

Kotter, John, 113–114, *114*

L

latent biases, 35–36

layoffs and termination, 73, 104, 130

leading vs. managing, 17–18

life services, 122

likeability, 71

litigation, 79

loyalty, 64, 66, 105

M

managers
  disengaged, 67–68
  employee career development plans, 49, 69
  employee perception of and engagement, 30
  listening and responsive action, 47
  micromanagement, avoidance of, 71
  multi-generational best practices, 61–64
  performance feedback, 49
  power of likeability, 71
  relationships and performance, 65–73
  of remote employees, 72, 122, 141
  role in employee engagement, 44–46, 132
  tools for employee motivation, 66, 70
  2013 State of the American Workplace (Gallup), 68
  as workplace bullies, 75
  See also specific aspects of engagement

managing vs. leading, 17–18

marketing
  to customers, 23–24
  employee engagement analogy, 23–25, 36–37, 44, 54–55, 95–96
  Packard on, 30

McKinsey Global Survey, on gender diversity and profitability, 32

measurement methods. *See* successful engagement, measurement of

mentoring, 41, 61–62, 72

micromanagement, 71

Microsoft, 134

military veterans. *See* veterans, stereotyping and

Millennial Branding, study on Gen Z, 59

Millennials. *See* Gen Y

minority groups. *See* ethnic minority groups

mission, communication of, 123–124

mission-driven orientation and continuous context (ENHANCE performance™ model), 106–107, 115

Mobility at Work program (Verizon Communications), 133

morale, 27, 34, 48

   See also workplace bullying

Morgan, Robert, 104

motivation. *See* employee motivation

MTV, study on creativity in workplace, 121

N

names of employees, 40

New Mothers Rooms (Microsoft), 134

New York Times, on workplace bullying, 78

O

on-boarding processes, 72

100 Best Companies (*Working Mother*), 133

100 Best Companies to Work For (*Fortune*), 125–127, 137

1:1 meetings, 47, 49

P

Packard, David, 30, 131

passively disengaged, defined, 27

pay and benefits programs, *Fortune's* selection criteria, 126

perceptions, in cultural gauge, 129

performance management and employee engagement, 95–101

   alignment with employees' goals, 99–100

   "Attracting and Retaining High-Technology Talent" survey, 99

   Gallup on employee attitudes and performance, 98–99

   GlobalWorkplaceAnalytics on remote employees, 100

   performance feedback, 49

   principles of, 96–97

relationships and performance, 65–73

remote work options, 100–101

teambuilding, 97–98

transparent salary models, 97–98

trust, 97

permanent positions, 109

Pittsburgh High Technology Council, "Attracting and Retaining High-Technology Talent" survey, 99

PricewaterhouseCoopers

   change management survey (2013), 88

   on generation gap in workplace, 64

pride and camaraderie, *Fortune's* selection criteria, 127

productivity and employee engagement, 29

   Blessing White, report on employee engagement (2013), 68

   career development plans, 69

   communications during change management, 89, 91

   disengaged employees impact on, 25–27

   in ENHANCE performance™ model, 110, 121–122

   Gallup on employee engagement, 46

   Gallup on lost productivity in US, 24, 117

   gender diversity and, 34–35

   managerial skills, 72

   peak age of, 105

   remote employee monitoring software and, 141

   restructuring, impact on, 109–110

   technology and, 105–106

   Towers Watson on employee commitment (2002), 46

   trust and, 45–46

   work-life integration and, 16

   See also generational groups, viewpoints of; performance management and employee engagement; profitability and employee engagement; workplace bullying

professional and personal development (ENHANCE performance™ model), 108–109, 116

profitability and employee engagement, 23–30, 68

   benefits of, 29

   Blessing White, report on employee engagement (2013), 24

technology. *See* digital technology

termination. *See* layoffs and termination

Towers Watson

    on employee commitment (2002), 46

    on profitability of engaged employees, 28

Traditionalists, 55, 59

training programs

    bullying prevention, 85–86

    communications, 35–36, 39–40, 108

    conflict management, 121

    diversity, 34, 35–36, 44, 121

    mentoring, 41

    professional development, 54

transparency, 47, 48

transparent salary models, 97–98

trust, 45–46, 47, 97, 120, 127

turnover, 37

turnover rates, 78

2013 State of the American Workplace (Gallup). *See* Gallup surveys

two-way mentoring, 61–62

U

Unilever, 133–134

United Parcel Service (UPS), 118

United States

    changing demographics of, 32

    lack of anti-bullying laws, 86

    lost productivity in, 24, 117

US Census Bureau, 32

V

Varian, 118

Verizon Communications, 133

veterans, stereotyping and, 85

virtual meetings, 121

W

walking meetings, 47

Warwick Business School, study on employee investment and stock valuation (2014), 126

Watson Wyatt WorkUSA Study (2208/2009), 46

websites

    company internal site, 108

    diversity information on, 41

    mission statements on, 123

Welsh, John J., 60

West Midland Family Center, 55

Wharton School, study on employee investment and stock valuation (2014), 126

William M. Mercer, Inc., "Attracting and Retaining High-Technology Talent" survey, 99

women

    family-friendly companies, 133–135

    gender diversity and profitability, 32, 34–35

    offensive stereotyping and, 81–83

    underrepresentation in technology companies, 53

    in workforce, 53

    workplace bullying, 78, 79–80

Women's Interactive Network (Unilever), 133

Working Hard Card, 62

Working Mother, 100 Best Companies, 133

work-life integration, 15–16, 100, 106, 116, 120–121

workplace bullying, 75–86

    behaviors of, 76–77

    business costs of, 75–76, 78–79

    contributing job factors, 80

    health impacts on victims of, 79, 80

    stereotyping and, 81–86

    WBTI on health impacts of, 78, 79–80, 85

    zero tolerance for, 86

Workplace Bullying & Trauma Institute (WBTI), 78, 79–80, 85

Worksnaps (software), 141

World Economic Forum, report on inheritance from Baby Boomer generation, 139

SCHEDULE A DIVERSITY TRAINING OR CORPORATE CIVILITY WORKSHOP WITH NICOLE MASON

THE SIMPLEST ACTION YOU can take to improve employee engagement is to schedule a training or workshop with Nicole. Her engaging trainings leave a lasting impression that effects positive changes, improves communication and facilitates diversity.

Call 510.468.3802 or visit

www.employeeandclientengagement.com/contact/

today, to schedule with Nicole

Additionally, you are invited to schedule a complimentary organizational performance assessment with Nicole. You can do that through the online meeting scheduler at: www.employeeandclientengagement.com/contact/ or email: Nicole@employeeandclientengagement.com.

Consulting Services:

Nicole Mason is the Founder of Omnivantage Business Professionals, a growth and change management consulting firm helping companies leverage diversity and develop employees, to improve overall performance.

QUICK BOOK ORDERS

Email orders: orders@truenorthpress.org

Telephone Orders: Call 1.408.479.4048. Have credit card ready.
If calling outside business hours, leave a message with your contact
information and your call will beturned.

Or visit: www.employeeandclientengagement.com/contact if you are
interested in ordering this book for your company or organization.

Request customized books for your company or organization:
Nicole@employeeandclientengagement.com

A complimentary keynote presentation by the author,
Nicole Mason, is available for organizations and companies
that special order customized copies of
ENHANCE Employee Engagement: Future Proof Company Strategies.

True North Press

Made in the USA
San Bernardino, CA
08 March 2015